TWAYNE'S WORLD AUTHORS SERIES

A Survey of the World's Literature

GREECE

Callimachus

TWAS 589

CALLIMACHUS

By JOHN FERGUSON

Selly Oak Colleges

TWAYNE PUBLISHERS

A DIVISION OF G. K. HALL & CO., BOSTON

Printed on permanent/durable acid-free paper and bound
in the United States of America

First Printing

Library of Congress Cataloging in Publication Data

Ferguson, John, 1921–
Callimachus.

(Twayne's world authors series ; TWAS 589 : Greece)
Bibliography: p. 175–79
Includes index.
1. Callimachus. 2. Authors, Greek—Biography.
PA3945.Z5F47   881'.01   80-16868
ISBN 0-8057-6431-3

FOR
R. P. S.

Contents

About the Author

John Ferguson, British classicist and theologian, was educated at Bishop's Stortford College and St. John's College, Cambridge. He has held university positions in Newcastle upon Tyne; London; Ibadan, Nigeria, and University of Minnesota. His visiting professorships include Hampton Institute, University of Florida and Ohio Wesleyan University. Having served as Dean and Director of Studies in Arts at Britain's Open University, he is now President of the Selly Oak Colleges in Birmingham, England.

The author of numerous articles in the fields of Greek philosophy, Greek tragedy, and Latin poetry and of about 50 books on classical and theological subjects, John Ferguson is also a well-known internationalist, serving as joint Editor of Reconciliation Quarterly, and chairman of Britain's United Nations Association.

Preface

I am glad of the opportunity to add *Callimachus* to *Aristotle* and *Clement of Alexandria* which I previously contributed to this series, and am grateful to Mary Gianos for her encouragement: she is much missed. There is no study of Callimachus in English, so I suppose it can be said that this "fills a gap." I have followed my previous practice: this is primarily a close guide through the poet's actual works, though this is complicated by the fact that their survival is so fragmentary. Callimachus is a seminal figure in the history of poetry, and it is important that more people have an opportunity to know about him in these Greekless days.

Rudolf Pfeiffer's great edition outmodes all others, and I have on the whole used that for the text. I have also used the convenient Loeb edition, A.W. Mair for *Hymns* and *Epigrams*, and C.A. Trypanis for the rest: Trypanis's notes are brilliant, and I have drawn extensively on them for the commentary. References are to the number of the poem or fragment and the line or lines in these standard editions.

The translations are all my own, and are taken from a forthcoming complete translation. So far as possible I let Callimachus speak for himself. For hexameters I use a form of sprung rhythm with a basic five word-beats to a line, varied occasionally to six or four. For elegiac couplets, following A.G. Lee's brilliant version of Ovid *Amores*, I have shortened the pentameter, even at the expense of Callimachus's line-structure. For the "limping iambics" I have tried to let the rhythm limp at the end. I have followed him in using alliteration or assonance in passages where it is prominent.

I was able to write the book on the hospitable campus of Ohio Wesleyan University in the winter of 1978. I am grateful to Mr. O.W. Carpenter for the endowment which made this possible, to Professor Samuel Pratt and his colleagues for their welcome, and to the Vice-Chancellor and Council of the Open University for releasing me for three months. Three other very warm expressions of gratitude are due, one to Karen Smith and all those who have performed the secretarial offices, the second to Kitty Chisholm for checking and constructive help, the third to my wife for her expert index-making.

JOHN FERGUSON

Selly Oak Colleges, England

Chronology

c245	Sosibius prominent. Approximate date for *Victory of Sosibius.*
c240	Revised edition of *Aitia* including "Lock of Berenice" and "Epilogue". Collected works.
c235	Callimachus dies.
221	Death of Ptolemy III. Murder of Berenice by Sosibius. *Terminus ad quem* for revised *Aitia.*

CHAPTER 1

Callimachus: His Life and Times

I The Hellenistic Age

IN 334 BC Alexander the Great of Macedon crossed the Hellespont and in so doing changed the world. In three years he crisscrossed over Asia Minor, swept down past Palestine to where Egypt was slumbering in the decay of her ancient glory, far into the desert to the oasis of Siwa where he had some kind of mystical experience, then back and around the Fertile Crescent to Babylon and Susa. Three great military victories routed the Persian armies. In the next seven years he pushed far into Asia, to the regions of Samarkand and Tashkent, then down into the Punjab, turning, because his troops would go no further, to the mouth of the Indus and back, enduring incredible privations along the coastal desert to Susa and Babylon.

He left behind the confined world of the city-state, the world of his tutor Aristotle, who declared that the non-Greek was by nature a slave, the world where men as enlightened as Socrates or Plato could thank the gods that they were born men not women, free men not slaves, Greeks not "barbarians." In this world Plato and Aristotle could insist that human beings had no natural existence except within the polis, the city-state, a relatively small, compact area both in geography and population, never exceeding about a quarter of a million people, and more often between 10,000 and 100,000 or even smaller: the tiniest territory of a city-state was no more than two square miles. Alexander pushed the horizons back. He mixed the nations together, as wine and water were mixed in a bowl. Small was no longer beautiful; men thought big. He created cosmopolis.

Alexander died tragically young, but the world of the city-state was not to return in its old form. His empire fragmented into warring kingdoms. For twenty years and more there was chaos as different aspirants sailed or marched to and fro around the eastern Mediterranean. Out of the chaos emerged three strong powers. One centered on Pella, the capital of Macedonia, and for the most part was able to maintain power in mainland Greece. Another had as its mainspring Syria, with its eventual capital at Antioch-on-the-Orontes. At first its power extended widely through Alexander's Asian conquests, but control was not possible and the more distant parts fell away, and by the middle of the third century Bactria had become an independent Greek kingdom, the Parthians had asserted their dominion in the old Persian Empire, and even in Asia Minor Pergamum had become the capital of a new power. The third, and stablest, of the dynasties was in Egypt.

These changes led to an identity-crisis in the Greek world. It was in fact by no means the end of the city-state. City-states flourished in the Hellenistic world as they were to do later under Rome. But it was a changed existence—changed in two interconnected ways. First, the existence of the individual had been largely defined by relation to his city: even cosmopolitan travelers like Protagoras or Hippias were known as "the man from Abdera" or "Hippias of Elis." The pushing back of the horizons left the citizen's existence undefined, uncircumscribed. Alongside this, he was no longer master of his destiny. The old city-state, whether oligarchy or democracy, was ruled by its citizens. Democracy was extended oligarchy, oligarchy contracted democracy; the relation of citizenship to government was the same. In the new world, authority was in Pella or Antioch or Alexandria or Pergamum, and local self-government, though real, was strictly limited: garrisons and taxes were reminders of where power lay. Furthermore, the new centers became the focal points of culture. Athens remained not negligible, especially in philosophy and drama. But Alexandria and Pergamum were the great cultural centers. The new capitals were on the way to becoming cities as we understand the term. Athens was the only classical city-state to approach this condition, and then perhaps only on the artificial conditions of wartime siege. But Alexandria was an urban complex, cosmopolitan, big enough to develop its own inner city problems. This was the environment of the Museum and Library and the new movement in literature.

II *Egypt*

After Alexander's death his chief officers had met at Babylon to determine the succession. Sovereignty devolved jointly on Alexander's mentally defective half-brother Philip III Arridaeus, and his posthumous son Alexander IV. Meantime, regency, which hardened into kingship, was essential. Egypt fell to a shrewd general named Ptolemy, who saw far before the others the power implicit in the situation. Further, by inventing a report that Alexander wished to be buried in the Oasis of Ammon he succeeded in securing the body for a tomb in his new capital of Alexandria. He extended his power by annexing Cyrene, to the west of Egypt, though that remained an uneasy acquisition. For a time he played expansionist military politics. He occupied Syria, lost it to Antigonus, and recovered it again. It was to be a bone of contention between the Ptolemies and the Seleucids throughout the third century. Not only so. Ptolemy secured Cyprus, lost it, and recovered it again. This remained Egyptian, providing an important naval base, through the third century: in the second century it again became a shuttlecock of power politics. Ptolemy further inched his way into Asia Minor, securing Pamphylia and Lycia, and, later, parts of Caria and the island of Cos. Ptolemy II made more conquests in Cilicia, but restored some parts to the Seleucids as part of a diplomatic initiative. But by the peace treaty of 241 the Ptolemies held power over nearly all of the coastal area of southern Asia Minor. The consequence of all this is that although Egypt was constantly at war in the power struggles of the third century, the wars were mostly far from her borders. Syria, Asia Minor, Greece, were all the constant scene of marching armies and raiding navies. Egyptian territory was by comparison inviolate.

This meant that the Egyptians were able to prosper economically. Max Cary called the first two Ptolemies "the greatest land-improvers in Greek history."[1] They maintained and restored existing irrigation channels. They developed a canal and sluice for conveying Nile water to the Fayum, and reclaimed so much land that a hundred new villages appeared there. Taxation was regulated so as to encourage irrigation. Many of the new farms were developed by Greek settlers. The Egyptian fellahin also received encouragement in their traditional methods, though the condition was supervision and control. Fruit farming increased; there was taxation relief for orchard development. Vines and olives were encouraged, and protected by an import tariff on rival products. Ranches began to develop a wool crop from pedigree animals imported from Miletus and elsewhere; this in turn led to the development of the textile industry in wool; linen weaving was maintained. Forestry was also developed for shipbuilding. There was already a high organization of village craft-guilds, and this continued under the Ptolemies. Mining was a government-controlled industry, and conditions were often brutal. Trade prospered. The magnificent harbor at Alexandria made possible the development of cargo boats up to 250 tons. Timosthenes under Ptolemy II wrote a guide to the harbors of the Mediterranean. Communications between the Nile and the Red Sea were improved.

The Ptolemaic court was a great center of culture. Ptolemy I early tried to induce Menander, the playwright, to leave Athens for Alexandria, but he would not do so. In 294 Ptolemy I invited the Aristotelian scholar Demetrius of Phalerum to establish an academy dedicated to the Muses, and himself appointed and paid the academic faculty. An extensive library was attached with perhaps half a million volumes by the middle of the century. Cultural activities including festivals abounded. Ptolemy II introduced a new festival, the Ptolemaea, in honor of his father. Musical performances developed on a scale unknown before. There was drama at the Ptolemaea, and a group of dramatists in Alexandria were known as the Pleiad, a term borrowed centuries later in France. Literature was encouraged and patronized, directly or indirectly. If we can trust the surface evidence of Callimachus's *Hymns,* various religious festivals might give opportunities for poetry as well as for music and dancing. Nor was this merely in Alexandria. Callimachus appears to be writing for Cyrene in some of his compositions. Ptolemais in Upper Egypt had its own dramatic company. Oxyrhynchus, no large town, supported poets and actors.

III   *Alexandria*

In 332 Alexander occupied the island of Pharos off the coast of Egypt, looked across to the coast where there was a fishing village named Rhacotis, and, seeing its potentialities for a city, instructed his architect Deinocrates to lay out a city. Deinocrates ran out of chalk and used barley to complete the plan. The birds swooped down to peck the grain. Alexander thought it a bad omen, but the quick-witted architect said that the new city would feed many others. The plan was the familiar grid, in this instance long and narrow, structured around two boulevards each thirty yards wide, crossing at right angles, one of them being the famous Canopic street.

It was a Greek city, with sections named after letters of the Greek alphabet. Rhacotis remained the district of the native Egyptians. The Jews had their own quarter. The Greeks settled in the Brucheum. Another section contained the official buildings. The island was connected to the mainland by a causeway, and had on it a lighthouse which was one of the wonders of the world, its lights perhaps intensified by a system of mirrors. The public buildings of the city were particularly impressive, the palaces looking out to sea, the museum and the library, the theater, stadium and hippodrome, the lawcourts and gymnasium, the Temple of Sarapis, the god who was virtually invented to meet the new ecumenical environment and to satisfy Jews and Greeks alike, and whose cult was to spread through the Graeco-Roman world. Another shrine of pilgrimage was the tomb which Ptolemy built for Alexander's body, around which as the years passed sprang up the temple-tombs of the deified Ptolemies.

Alexander did not live to see the completion of the greatest of all the numerous Alexandrias, properly called Alexandria-by-Egypt to emphasize a certain apartness from the Egyptian scene, but Ptolemy endorsed his choice of site by taking it as his capital. It prospered into a busy cosmopolis. "The other cities," says one writer, "are cities in relation to the surrounding countryside, but villages in relation to Alexandria, which is the city of the world."[2] We have a vivid picture of its bustling, jostling mobs on a festival occasion in Theocritus's fifteenth idyll:

GORGO: Heavens, what a mob! It's ghastly, how can we
           get through? There's no end to them—just like ants.
PRAXINOA: Ptolemy, that's one of the best things you've done
           since your father went off to the sky. There are
           no hoods creeping up as you pass and doing you
           in—a good old Egyptian habit.
           None of those old tricks, the devils,
           all the same, all dirty, all Bolshies—

Gorgo darling, what'll become of us? It's the King's
Own Cavalry. Please, sir, don't run me down.
Look at that bay rearing; he's furious. Eunoa,
don't be a damned fool, get out of the way (15, 44-54).

IV   *The Museum and Library*

The Museum, or Shrine of the Muses, the "hen-coop" of the
Muses, as it was satirically called, was founded by Demetrius of
Phalerum in 294 on Aristotelian principles. It expanded into a
large university complex, including lecture halls, seminar rooms,
and roofed walks where the Peripatetic practices of teaching
could be continued. There were botanical and zoological gardens
and an observatory. The greatest achievements of the Alex-
andrians were arguably in the field of science, especially
mathematics, astronomy, and medicine. It was at the Museum
that under Ptolemy I Euclid wrote *The Elements* which was
destined to have the longest life of any textbook in history. It was
here too that Apollonius of Perge developed the theory of conic
sections, that Archimedes under Ptolemy III and Heron later
applied mathematical theory to engineering and invented the
waterscrew and a rudimentary steam engine. In astronomy
Eratosthenes invented the armillary sphere, and Aristarchus
developed the heliocentric theory, anticipating Copernicus by
more than a millennium and a half. In medicine Herophilus of
Chalcedon watched autopsies and extended the knowledge of
anatomy and physiology thereby. Erasistratus of Iulis seems to
have used vivisection to the same end.
The Museum was a convenient place to attach the writers
whom the Ptolemies attracted to their court. It was in the urban
environment that Theocritus developed the forms of pastoral
poetry as a form of escape. Callimachus and Apollonius were
certainly placed by their royal patron in the Museum. The Muses
who presided over science were the inspiration of poets. We
should not forget when Callimachus invokes the Muses that it is
no mere literary artifice, since he was a member of the staff of
the Muses' own temple.
For those with a literary bent the Library, which grew in
association with the Museum, was a useful center, and
Callimachus and Apollonius certainly had official duties there.
The number of volumes (in the form of papyrus rolls) rose by

mid-second century to about half a million. Ptolemy III was responsible for securing copies of the great Athenian tragedies. According to the story told by Galen, he secured a loan of the official state copies against a large deposit, had a magnificent transcript made—and returned the transcript, forfeiting his deposit. He also confiscated any foreign books arriving in Alexandria, having copies made for the unfortunate owners. As the library expanded, a second branch, with some 42,900 volumes was introduced at the Temple of Sarapis. The presence of so much research material led to a certain amount of dry but useful research in bibliography, linguistic usage, textual criticism, grammar and syntax, and the like. More, George Sarton has suggested a close parallelism between the development of grammar and anatomy—the anatomy of language and the anatomy of the human body advancing side by side.[3]

Callimachus was closely associated with the Library, and responsible for the great catalogue. But for some reason he was passed over in the succession for the chief librarian, and his junior and student Apollonius of Rhodes was appointed. The evidence is complex but clear. The first librarian was Zenodotus of Ephesus, an epic poet. A papyrus from Oxyrhynchus (1241) gives a list of librarians: Apollonius of Rhodes, Eratosthenes, Aristophanes of Byzantium, Apollonius the idographer, Aristarchus. It is possible that we should put Apollonius the idographer before Aristophanes, but otherwise the succession is well established. Now Tzetzes says more than once that Aristarchus was fourth or fifth in succession from Zenodotus. These statements together make it impossible to fit Callimachus into the list, and as there is no statement to the contrary which may not be a loose expression of his undoubted association with the library, this clinches the matter. We must suspect a fair amount of academic politics behind his exclusion, though our surviving poems show no bitterness on his part in direct relation to this; in an autocratic court that would have been injudicious.

V   *Cyrene*[4]

In myth the eponymous goddess of the city of Cyrene was a nymph, daughter of Hypseus. She was a creature of the mountains. Apollo saw her one day when she was grappling with a lion, fell in love with her strength and beauty, and carried her

off to Africa where he fathered Aristaeus on her. In another
version the local king was named Eurypylus. His kingdom was
being devastated by a ferocious lion; he offered the throne as a
reward for killing the animal. Cyrene accomplished this and
received the kingdom. She was evidently associated with lion-
killing. In some versions she bore Apollo another son, who stayed
behind in Libya, when Aristaeus left.

The foundation-story is told by Pindar, Herodotus, Lycophron,
and Apollonius. The story is linked with the myth of the
Argonauts. They were driven by gales into the Syrtes, landed on
the coast of Africa, where Euphemus was presented with a lump
of African soil by Eurypylus. This fell overboard and was washed
up at Thera. Medea with her witchery foretold that descendants
of Euphemus would come to Thera, and one of them, Battus,
would establish a colony in Libya. Euphemus settled in Lemnos,
but his descendants were driven out and settled near Sparta.
When Theras was seeking colonists for Calliste (to be renamed
Thera), he took with him some of these refugees. Eventually,
acting under instructions from Delphi, Battus led a group to the
African coast. They first settled on an island off the coast, then
on the mainland at Aziris or Azilis (at the mouth of the Wadi
Khalij) before they eventually moved to what became Cyrene,
where they settled by Apollo's Spring and the Myrtle-hill (the
region is rich in myrtles). Callimachus's second hymn typically
alludes to many of the episodes and places associated with these
traditions.

Cyrene maintained its independence from Egypt in the decay
of the old order. But when Egypt was taken over by a freshly
dynamic dynasty, Greek and actively imperialistic, the situation
changed. Alexander himself did not move further west along the
coast, but Cyrene took care to send him a suitably deferential
embassy. But at much the time that Ptolemy was establishing
himself in Egypt, Cyrene was suffering from the *stasis* or internal
conflict which was the bane of the Greek city-states. The losing
party called in a Spartan mercenary named Thibron, who was
himself engaged in a leadership struggle in his own forces.
Thibron besieged Cyrene. There were further internal
upheavals leading to a radical democratic revolution; the rich
escaped either to Thibron or to Ptolemy, who was interesting
himself in the situation for his own ends. Thibron's forces and

those inside the city succeeded in reaching an accommodation, but Ptolemy sent an army under Ophellas, who won a military victory, killing Thibron, and established himself as governor of Cyrene in the name of Ptolemy. Ptolemy himself visited the city in 322.

For nearly ten years there was a measure of stability. We have the terms of settlement, though it is not quite clear whether they date from 322 or 308. In general, the traditional structure with Cyrene as a city-state, and the center of the Cyrenaic League, was maintained. But Ptolemy reserved to himself certain privileges associated with the granting of citizenship and the restoration of exiles, the appointment of the Senate, and his own position as *strategos*, military commander and magistrate. Then in 313 Cyrene revolted and drove out Ophellas. Temporarily only; he was soon reinstated. But now Ophellas himself started acting independently, and made a personal alliance with Agathocles in Sicily. This new move was dangerous to Ptolemy who watched with some apprehension. But in 309 Agathocles and Ophellas fell out, and Ophellas was murdered. Ptolemy now sent his stepson Magas to recover Cyrene.

Magas was a remarkable man, even from the little we know of him. He was Ptolemy's stepson and viceroy, but Ptolemy was never certain of his loyalty. For a quarter of a century we hear little of Cyrene. With the succession of Ptolemy II the situation became more unstable. Antiochus the Seleucid was trying to weaken the power of Egypt, and it was probably under his influence that Magas revolted in 274. He marched towards Egypt with an army, but was checked and recalled by news of a rising of the Marmaridae, one of the desert tribes. Some suspicious historians have supposed that this rising was deliberately engineered; Magas was playing a double game, and had to make a show of force against Ptolemy, but the last thing he wanted was a full-scale war with Ptolemy. Ptolemy and Magas came to terms. War was averted, and for another quarter century there was relative stability and tranquillity, Cyrene enjoying a fair measure of practical independence.

We have from Strabo, quoted by Josephus,[5] a picture of Cyrene and Cyrenaica under the Ptolemies. It was not dissimilar from Alexandria and Egypt. The capital was a Greek city, with a large non-Greek population, especially Jews, and of course native Libyans. The farmland was in the possession either of the king or of the city; the farmers entrusted with its cultivation and protection were probably ex-soldiers.

Somewhere in the early 250s Magas betrothed his daughter Berenice to a Ptolemy, possibly but not certainly the future Ptolemy III. The period of betrothal was long and drawn-out. Magas in time of peace "gave himself over to pleasures," becoming so fat that he was eventually suffocated by his own grossness. He was a skilled ruler, whose name appears on one of the monuments of the great Asoka far away in India. After his death Cyrene immediately became the prey of the power politicians. One named Demetrius the Fair, an Antigonid and a grandson of Ptolemy I, came to Cyrene, seeing marriage with Berenice as a way to power. If the princess still had ties with Egypt, she now broke them and became affianced to Demetrius. But Demetrius had an affair with Berenice's mother. Berenice scorned was a hellcat, and had him killed. The situation in Cyrene broke into the wranglings of party politics. In about 251 two liberators from Megalopolis, with Platonic connections, Ecdemus and Demophanes, were called in, and reorganized the old League. It was not to last. There were active hostilities with Egypt. All this was resolved with the death of Ptolemy II, the succession of Ptolemy III Euergetes, and his marriage to Berenice, all in 247. Egypt and Cyrene were now united under a single dynasty, and were to remain so united for the rest of Callimachus's life at least. Euhesperides was now called Berenice, Teucheira Arsinoe, Barce Ptolemais, and the coinage restruck to glorify Ptolemy.

The archaeological remains, mostly a Roman reworking of the Hellenistic city, are still impressive. The site is uneven, so that the grid pattern is irregular. There is one major street on the NE-SW axis, crossed by three streets at right angles. The famous tomb of Battus stands by the ancient agora. Around are stoas and temples among which the Capitolium and Temple of Demeter are prominent. The latter housed a colossal statue. Further east is the Roman forum with a small Temple of Bacchus in the center, a Hellenistic odeon, and a Roman theater. The fountain and sanctuary of Apollo form an area of particular historical interest. The largest of all the temples is that of Zeus; but in its present form it is of the Roman period. Outside the city is an extensive necropolis, with rock-cut tombs going back to the sixth century B.C. and accommodation for many thousands of dead.

VI *Callimachus's Life*

Our principal source of information about Callimachus's uneventful life comes from the notice in the late biographical compilation *The Suda:*

Callimachus, son of Battus and Mesatma, of Cyrene, grammarian, pupil of Hermocrates of Iasos, the grammarian, married the daughter of Euphraeus of Syracuse. His sister had a son, Callimachus the younger, author of an epic *On Islands.* He was so industrious that he wrote poems in every meter as well as a large number of prose works: the books he wrote add up in all to more than eight hundred. He lived in the reign of Ptolemy Philadelphus. Before his introduction to that king he was a teacher of grammar in Eleusis, a small suburb of Alexandria. He survived into the reign of Ptolemy named Euergetes and Olympiad 127, in the second year of which Ptolemy Euergetes began to reign.

The notice, unfortunately, is not wholly reliable, being demonstrably wrong in one point and probably in two others; at the same time it preserves information we should not otherwise have.

Callimachus came from Cyrene, an independent Greek colony uneasily in the Egyptian sphere of influence, as we have seen. His father's name was Battus. This was the name of the founder of the colony, and we know from Strabo (17,837) that Callimachus claimed descent from the original Battus. However that may be, his family was prominent in Cyrene, and his grandfather Callimachus was an outstanding general. His mother's name was probably not Mesatma, but Megatima: certainly that was his sister's name according to *The Suda*'s notice of his nephew. At his date of birth we can only guess. The only additional evidence we have is that he was a little younger than Aratus. A reasonable guess for his birth would be about 310.

The life of Aratus tells us that the two studied together with an Aristotelian philosopher named Praxiphanes, presumably in Alexandria, as Callimachus seems never to have traveled by sea (fr. 178,32). It is likely to have been here that he worked with Hermocrates, who had the dubious distinction of being an

authority on accents. We will sensibly place this period of study
in the 280s. Alexandria was already becoming the new cultural
capital of the Greek world. Some of Callimachus's epigrams
indicate a period of poverty. This may mean that there had been
a change of fortune in his family; or it may have been that he had
come to the great city determined to stand on his own feet.
There is no reason to doubt *The Suda*'s statement that he spent a
period grinding away at the work of schoolteaching in the
suburbs of the capital till such time as he was able to attract the
emperor's attention. The exact form the emperor's patronage
took is obscure. But it seems that Callimachus was officially
attached in some capacity to the Royal Library, and the evidence
of Tzetzes is that he was still young at the time. It can be taken as
quite certain that he was never Chief Librarian, but the
traditions suggest that he played a useful part in the cataloguing.
The Suda associates his career with the reign of Ptolemy
Philadelphus, who became joint ruler with his father in 285, and
sole ruler in 283. It is difficult to distinguish poems written with
an eye on court appointments from those written out of court
appointments, but the hymns show an awareness of imperial
patronage. They were all written after 283, and the oldest
probably not very long after. The references to the poet's youth
suggest that by the early 270s, if not before, he was established
in imperial favor.

   The Suda's eight hundred works is an exaggeration—unless
individual poems and sections of longer poems such as *Aitia* are
counted separately. *The Suda* names some twenty-four titles as
"included in his works." These begin with six not known from
other sources: *The Coming of Io, Semele, Settlements of Argos,
Arcadia, Glaucus, Hopes.* Of these nothing is known. They might
be lost sections of *Aitia; The Settlements of Argos* recalls both
"The Fountains of Argos" and "On the Sicilian Cities." Or they
might be lyrics. *The Coming of Io* and *Semele* would be excellent
subjects for epyllia, short stories in the epic idiom. There is a
tradition that his best-known epyllion, *Hecale,* was written in
answer to critics, to show that he could do it, but he may have
written others before or after: *Galatea* was one such. *The Suda*
then has four collections, *Satyric Plays, Tragedies, Comedies* and
Lyrics. Of the first three nothing is known. There is no reason
why the poet should not have tried his hand at drama, but if he

wrote extensively it is slightly odd that they are sunk without trace. On the other hand, the summaries of his collected works place four lyric poems between *Iambi* and *Hecale*, three of which are mentioned elsewhere. Next comes *Ibis*, a celebrated hymn of hate. It is curious that the selection omits such well-known poems as *Aitia*, *Hecale*, *The Lock of Berenice*, and the collections of *Iambi*, *Hymns*, and *Epigrams*, as well as other lesser elegies or epyllia, well-known in their day.

We may reasonably assume that the remainder of the titles cited in *The Suda* are prose works. We shall discuss these briefly later. The first three perhaps refer to the same work: *The Museum, Catalogue of Writers eminent in all fields of literature and of their Works, Catalogue and Chronological List of Dramatic Poets from the beginning of Drama* (presumably a section of the full *Catalogue*). The other titles show the variety of his interests: *Dictionary of the Language and Compositions of Democritus* (perhaps an offshoot of the *Catalogue*), *Local Names of Months, Foundations and Changes of Name of Islands and Cities, The Rivers of Europe, Unusual Marvels in the Peloponnese and Italy, Different Names of Fishes, Winds, Birds, The Rivers of the World, Encyclopaedia of Worldwide Marvels arranged geographically.* A few titles, probably of prose works, are known from other sources. Most important of these is *Local Nomenclature* which probably subsumes some of the titles given in *The Suda*. *The Rivers of Asia* will be a subsection of the larger book. Other titles are *On the Eyes, The Customs of Foreigners, The Nymphs, Against Praxiphanes*, and *Historical Notes*.

Till this century all that survived of this vast corpus consisted of six *Hymns*, sixty-four *Epigrams*, a Latin translation (by Catullus) of *The Lock of Berenice*, and scores of phrases quoted out of context. A great impulse to the study of Callimachus has come within this century through discoveries of papyri in Egypt. These include substantial fragments of some of the otherwise lost poems, notably *Aitia* and *Hecale*, his two most celebrated poems in antiquity. This find enables us to attain a much juster view of his achievement. In addition to the fragments, which have received the attention of a number of great scholars (Callimachus has been well served by scholarship, for Richard Bentley and Wilamowitz, the towering geniuses, in different centuries, of British and German classical scholarship, made

major contributions to his study), above all that of Rudolf
Pfeiffer, we have valuable information from three *Diegeseis* or
Summaries, all derived from a single lost source, which help us to
see the story behind some of the tantalizing fragments.

The poems do a little to enable us to fix the dates of
Callimachus's working life. Negatively we can say that there is
no indication of any poem earlier than about 283, except that the
epigrams complaining of poverty probably belong to the 280s.
Pfeiffer would place *Epigram* 20, written at Cyrene, even
earlier; perhaps also *Epigram* 54. There are reasons for thinking
that *Hymn* 1 (not the first to be written) belongs to the period
283–280. References to the incursion of the Gauls into the Greek
world must be after 278; these are in *Hymn* 4 and *Galatea. The
Deification of Arsinoe* must be after the queen's death in 270; so
must the reference in *Hymn* 4 to the deification of Ptolemy II. At
the other end, *The Lock of Berenice* must be after the events in
247–6 which it describes, and *The Victory of Sosibius* can hardly
be before about 245. We have one more clue. At some point the
poet organized an edition of his collected poetry. For this he
incorporated *The Lock of Berenice* in *Aitia,* and added an
epilogue leading the reader on to *Iambi.* This may—it does not
always—indicate that he had given up writing. In any case it will
hardly have been before about 240, and it cannot have been
after the murder of Berenice by Sosibius in 221. It is unlikely that
the poet survived to see that. *The Suda's* date for his death
(272–269) is hopelessly wrong. The most obvious emendation
would make the text refer to Olympiad 133 (248–245). This
would be right for Ptolemy Euergetes, but it seems early for the
poet's death. The entry may mean that the compiler knew that
the poet survived into the new reign, but had no information
beyond. *The Suda* entry for Aristophanes of Byzantium contains
a slight suggestion that Callimachus outlived Zenodotus, whose
death was probably 245–235. A reasonable guess would put his
death to about 240–235, between the age of 70 and 75, and the
issue of the collected poems a little before that. His working life
thus spanned about forty-five years.

Callimachus stood for a distinctive literary viewpoint. It is
familiarly expressed in one of the most famous anecdotes of
antiquity, recorded by Athenaeus (2,72 A): "Callimachus the
schoolteacher used to say that a big book is equivalent to a big

evil." The remark is slightly puzzling. It may be an aesthetic judgment of the appropriate length of a literary work. It may be a librarian's comment on the awkwardness of handling unwieldy scrolls; Callimachus's own scrolls did not much exceed a thousand lines. It may be a schoolmaster's comment on the boredom of going through seemingly unending works in the schoolroom. And we may recall that it was another Hellenistic writer who said "Of making many books there is no end" (*Eccl.* 12: 12).

Whatever the point of this remark, Callimachus stood for two important principles, both clearer in their negative form, "Avoid excessive length" and "Avoid well-trodden paths." Both appear in a couplet which begins an epigram.

> I hate epic poetry. I take no pleasure in a road
>   leading crowds here and there. (28, 1–2)

That, he says, is prostitution of art. The same two principles come in the curious passage which ends the second *Hymn*. Broad rivers carry much flotsam and jetsam; the gods prefer a stream that is slender and pure. Callimachus reasserts them again at the end of his life in the new preface to *Aitia*, where Apollo gives him two instructions: to keep his Muse slim, and to keep his car off the high roads. So he espouses Hesiod as a model rather than Homer, and brings a strong lyrical impulse, derived from Alcaeus and particularly Pindar, to bear on epic subjects. He perfects too the epyllion, the epic episode, the miniature epic: it is his demonstration of the way to treat epic subjects without the sprawling, shapeless bulk (as he viewed it) of epic. Positively he believed in learning, carried to such an extent that much of his poetry may have impressed but can hardly have attracted the ordinary hearer. Yet he knew too how to blend together with his learned allusiveness direct writing, simple conversational language, genre pictures of ordinary life as characteristic of their age as Myrine figurines, exciting adventures. In fact, to be what the Romans later called *doctus poeta,* a learned poet, was not just a matter of scholarship, but of mastery of meter and language of all sorts, and a capacity to arouse admiration by variety and ingenuity. Philitas of Cos, a poet of whom we know little, was his exemplar in subtleties of poetry.

Callimachus was a scholar. The list of his known prose works
alone suggests a combination of wide academic interests and
close attention to detail. We know of a number of his "students"
(whatever exactly that may mean). They include two of the most
eminent scholars of the day, Eratosthenes and Aristophanes.
Eratosthenes came from Callimachus's native Cyrene, a man of
such width of interest that he was nicknamed Beta, number two
in any field you mention. We can see Callimachus's influence in
that breadth of outlook. But Eratosthenes was a man of real
distinction, especially in mathematics and astronomy; he established the basis of Greek chronology, and calculated the
circumference of the earth with a remarkable degree of
precision. He also wrote poetry in a broadly Callimachean
manner. Aristophanes came from Byzantium. He left his mark on
literary history by inventing the written accent and generally
systematizing punctuation: he was also an outstanding editor, not
least in lyric poetry, analyst, and lexicographer. Pfeiffer
regarded him as the chief representative of Alexandrian
scholarship at its height. Another student was Apollonius,
nicknamed the Rhodian. It is possible that he studied with
Callimachus as an apprentice. In literature he was no slavish
disciple of Callimachus; he was interested enough in learning,
and in human psychology, but he believed that the Homeric
tradition was still valid, and the story that they fell out over this
is intrinsically probable, even if we discount the tendency of
later critics to refer any hostile aside in Callimachus to
Apollonius. The evidence is limited and conflicting. There is a
tradition that the invective *Ibis* was directed against Apollonius,
but the scholia do not include him in the Telchines whom
Callimachus attacks in *Aitia*. One tradition says that Apollonius
turned to poetry late, after leaving Callimachus, another that his
Argonautica was an early work and a humiliating failure, and
that he retired to Rhodes to revise it, and returned to an
important post in the Museum. We are even told that the two
poets were buried together.

We have then the picture of a buried life (as was said of A.E.
Housman, another scholar-poet). A man of many parts, grammarian and teacher, librarian and bibliophile, scholar, poet,
Callimachus was seemingly a younger contemporary of two of
the other major poets, Aratus, whose learning and poetic gifts he

approved, and Theocritus, and an older contemporary of Apollonius, whom he may have outlived. We do not know his relation to Philitas of Cos, who is later named with him. All these poets made their individual contributions to poetic style, but Callimachus, more than any other, stands as representative of his age.

CHAPTER 2

Aitia

I Explanations

AITIA or *Explanations* was Callimachus's most famous poem in antiquity. Euripides, the tragic dramatist, had shown some interest in correlating myth and ritual, and other writers evince some curiosity about the origins of cultic practices and other unusual customs, but it seems likely that Callimachus was the first to essay a systematic exposition in the form of a collection of such explanations or origins. For a poet who espoused the short poem, and averred as much in introducing his great work, it seems that the original was of surprising length, extending to 7000 or more lines: this is longer than Apollonius's *The Voyage of the Argonauts.* But Callimachus's is in no real sense an extended poem. It is a series of charms strung along a bracelet, or jewels in a necklace, each quite small, carefully shaped, and highly polished. There is no consistent theme in any individual book. Callimachus had studied with the Aristotelian Praxiphanes, but in this use of discontinuous form he was striking out along his own lines. This technique was one aspect of the poem's influence. Ovid's *Fasti* is close to *Aitia* in structure and approach; his *Metamorphoses* is based on the same principle. One of the more characteristic products of the Hellenistic Age was the medley of prose and verse known as Menippean satire, after Menippus of Gadara. This too strung together loosely connected units. Even prose novels, such as the Latin *Metamorphoses* of Apuleius, are similarly constructed.

The other influential aspect of *Aitia* was the poet's learning. The "learned poet" of later generations was the absolute master of poetic technique, but he was also the purveyor of out-of-the-way information. Such learning is characteristic of much Latin poetry, and is by no means confined to the later "Silver" authors.

To hold together a poem of 7000 lines in which the subject-matter is antiquarian, and the sections essentially similar, is no facile task. Even with only a fragment of the whole we can see some of the ways in which Callimachus faced this challenge. First, his verse has much charm. Even unpromising proper names are turned to sonorous effect. Lines of indirect allusiveness are varied with vividly clear statement: see, for example, the single line on Athens:

> No other town knows how to pity. (51)

Alliteration and assonance are used with careful husbandry. Above all, Callimachus shows total command of rhythmic variety: the elegiac couplet allows subtle effects here. One example will suffice. It comes in his account of the founding of the cities of Sicily. The Muse is telling the story of Perieres and Crataemenes. They land in Sicily—in a rush of dactyls (the verse spills over from one couplet to another)—and then they are brought up short because they have taken no precautions against a mysterious bird of prey, which is described in heavy spondees as "hostile to builders" (43,58-62).

Secondly, Callimachus diversifies the subjects of his *Explanations.* He includes explanations of the use of blasphemous words in offering sacrifice on Rhodes, or of the lamb festival at Argos; the delightful love story of Acontius and Cydippe; curious accounts of Hera's statues at Samos; the cautionary tale of the boastful huntsman; a story from Roman history; and the legendary *Lock of Berenice.*

Thirdly, there is his wit, the wit, for example, in *Molorchus* in which Callimachus told of the Nemean lion which Heracles killed:

> Zeus's bad-tempered wife
> sent him to ravage her own land of Argos, for Zeus's illegitimate
> son a tough task. (55)

A bit later (57) the poet suggests that the reader can skip the rest and make up his own answers—but the poem goes on. *The Lock of Berenice* is delightful in its wit. The Lock takes an oath by the

head and life of the queen that it did not mean to be cut off.
When iron can dig a canal through Mt. Athos, what chance has a
mere lock of hair? (110)

Fourthly, Callimachus is always ready to bring in a tinge of
realism, an eye-witness observation, a personal touch. He may
make Simonides speak from the tomb, but he addresses Acontius
in his own voice. He may converse with the Muses, and allow
them to tell him what he should say, but when he writes of the
cities of Sicily he makes clear when he is speaking from his own
experience. He is not afraid to add reflections of his own:

> Men grow old gracefully
> when young lads love them like their own parents,
> escorting them home. (41)

II   The Introductory Poem

We do not know exactly when Callimachus wrote *Aitia*. An
ancient commentator says that he was "quite young"; certainly
the poem achieved a firm reputation in the poet's lifetime. We
may reasonably deduce that he revised the poem for inclusion in
his collected verse towards the end of his life, though he possibly
did not alter the text of the main body of the poem drastically, as
we have no indication of variant readings beyond what we would
expect in the normal wear-and-tear of manuscript copying. At
this time he added an independently published poem, *The Lock
of Berenice*, modifying it to suit the sequence, and an epilogue
leading to the next part of the collected verse, *Iambics*.

At this point also he added an introduction "Against the
Telchines," which he intended as an prooemium both to *Aitia*
and to his poetry as a whole, and as a mature and definitive
account of his approach to poetry. The Telchines were
legendary workers in metal, and magicians. Callimachus uses the
term for his literary opponents, whom he regards as monstrous
anachronisms, workers in a heavy medium unlike his more
delicate filigree, and practitioners of black and hostile sorcery.
The passage, although fragmentary, is important enough to be
cited in full.

Of course the Telchines growl at my song—
  ignoramuses, the Muses' enemies—
because I did not extend a single poem through many thousand
  lines to sing of kings
or valiant heroes, preferring to get out a brief story
  like a child, for all my years.
I have some words of wisdom for the Telchines
  "You tribe of heart-wasters,
you scorn the man of few lines, but Demeter's grace
  counts for far more than massive. . . .
Of the two rivals, the delicate one showed the delights of Mimnermus,
  not the Fat Lady.
Flights from Egypt to the country of Thrace
  are for pygmy-gorged cranes.
Long-distance shots at the Persians are the province of the Massagetae.
  Nightingales sing sweetest being small.
Off with you, deathly family of jealousy. Judge poetry
  by technique not length.
Don't look to me to give birth to bawling songs:
  thunder is for Zeus not me."
When I first got a writing-block on my knee
  Apollo said to me:
"My poetic friend, feed up your sacrifices to fatness,
  keep your Muse slim.
One further instruction: travel away from the main roads,
  don't drive your car along routes
used by others, avoid broad highways, take unfrequented tracks,
  even if you find them narrow.
My audience is those who love the cicadas' shrill chirping
  and loathe the din of donkeys."
Others can bray like that long-eared brute; let me be
  the light winged creature—
yes indeed, let my song be sustained by dewdrops,
  the divine air's free nourishment;
let me put off old age, which weighs me down
  like Sicily on Enceladus.
No cause for worry! If the Muses smile on one in youth,
  they do not turn away from his gray hairs. (1)

    The references are not wholly clear. Mimnermus was a writer
of elegiac love poetry in the seventh century B.C., the archetype
of the love poet. He fell in love with a flute-girl from Lydia

named Nanno. She may have been the slender recipient of
slender poems, and contrasted with *Lyde*, a grossly inflated
poem by Antimachus, which Catullus, Callimachus's Roman
disciple, refers to with critical disapproval. *Demeter* was a poem
by another contemporary, one whom Callimachus admired,
Philitas of Cos; their names were to be linked together as models
by the Roman Propertius. Demeter's massive rival cannot be
recovered, but it will again be a poem by an overexpansive
contemporary. The far-flying cranes (their war with the Pygmies
was a favorite myth) and the far-shooting Massagetae, and the
vast estates of Persia (and Egypt), and thunder rolling through
the whole sky, and fleshy animals, are all symbols of what poetry
in Callimachus's view should not be. His own poems are
"nightingales," a word he applied to those of his friend
Heraclitus.

Having established his first point, concision, the poet passes to
a second, originality, neatly expressed by imagery from travel.
But this too links with the former image, for untraveled ways are
also narrow. He sums the matter up in a brilliant image, the cicala
contrasted with the donkey. The cicala in Mediterrean and
tropical lands makes a friendly sound by rubbing its legs
together: the light but penetrating "song" is excellently set
against the braying of asses. The cicala was the favorite of the
Muses[1], and other Alexandrian poets use the comparison[2].
Further, the cicala was regarded as immortal. Tithonus, human
husband to the divine Dawn, asked for the gift of immortality but
forgot to ask for eternal youth and withered into a cicala; but
Callimachus sees the cicala as sloughing off old age, which the
poet says presses on him as Sicily presses on the giant Enceladus
who was imprisoned thereunder for challenging the power of
Zeus.

This introduction thus is not merely Callimachus's apology for
his life and work, it is also a demonstration of it.

III   *The First Book*

With this introduction we pass to the body of the work. An
episode called "The Dream" told how the great Boeotian poet
Hesiod was inspired by the Muses. Even the fragments that
survive—less than five lines in all—show us Callimachus's

technique. There is learned allusion: the spring Hippocrene, caused in myth when the winged steed Pegasus stamped his hoof, is called "the hoofprint of the high-mettled horse." There is irony: the Muses are described as "a swarm." There is moralism, as when Callimachus picks up a line of Hesiod and declares that "to harm another is to harm oneself."[3] The section went on to Callimachus's own claims to inspiration. It will be noted that he does not claim Homeric inspiration: Hesiod is his master, the Hesiod who in *The Theogony* set out the pattern of Greek myth. The passage was vastly famous; it was much imitated, and an epigram by Diodorus has it for theme:

Famed Dream of Battus's learned son,
    you were clearly of horn not ivory.
You displayed to us things we men had not before known
    about gods and demigods,
when you carried him from Africa to Helicon
    setting him amongst the Muses.
They replied to his questions on Explanations about the primeval
    heroes and blessed gods. (*AP* 7,42)

It is ironical that in his account of the poet who rejected Homer Diodorus should advert to a passage in *The Odyssey,* where Dreams which pass through the Gate of Ivory are deceitful, those which pass through the Gate of Horn are true (Hom. *Od.* 19,562-7).

Next came "The Graces." According to some traditions they were children of Zeus, by Hera or Eurynome or Euanthe; but Callimachus preferred a myth which ascribed their birth to Dionysus and a nymph named Coronis. The islanders of Paros used to sacrifice to the Graces without the accompaniment of flutes or garlands. Why? Callimachus went for his answer to an ancient compiler of legendary history named Agias, whose work was revised by one of the Alexandrian scholars named Dercylus[4]. According to the story they told, Minos, king of Crete, was on Paros making sacrifice to the Graces when a messenger arrived with news of his son's death. Minos very properly completed the ritual, but as a sign of grief took off the garland he was wearing and stopped the flute music. Callimachus produced a splendid line to describe Cretan naval imperialism:

and Minos laid a heavy yoke along the islands' neck. (4)

He ended with a description of the Graces in their beauty and a
prayer for their help:

Come now, and shed the benediction of your hands on my elegies,
that they may last for many years. (7, 13-4)

Callimachus followed this directly with "The Return of the
Argonauts and the Rite of Anaphe." Here we can see more
clearly the dramatic framework of his episodes. He asks his
question of the Muses and one of the Muses replies. Here the
question was why on the small isle of Anaphe shocking language
was used in the worship of Apollo. This must have been a longish
episode for it involved an extended account of the adventures of
Jason and the Argonauts, the theme of his rival Apollonius
Rhodius's *Argonautica*. Anaphe was a refuge to which Apollo,
under the title of Aegletes, Radiant, the gleam piercing the
darkness from a distance, had directed the travelers in a storm.
With them they had twelve Phaeacian girls, a present from the
queen of Phaeacia to Medea. As the heroes made their sacrifice
of thanksgiving for deliverance, these girls started giggling. The
Argonauts told them off, they answered back, and a slanging-
match, no doubt with plenty of sexual innuendo, ensued. This
became a part of the ritual[5].

This led naturally to an account of another sacrifice offered to
Heracles at Lindus on the island of Rhodes, in the course of
which blasphemous language was used. Any ritual involving such
language was in later times popularly known as "Lindian
sacrifice" or "Rhodian sacrifice." The story behind this was that
Heracles near Lindus met "a cultivator cutting the furrow for
seed" (22) and asked him for food. The man surlily refused; so
Heracles killed one of the man's oxen and ate it, while the man
produced a remarkable string of blasphemies. From Callimachus
one curse only remains: "May you feed off flesh bitter as bile!"
(530). He called the lost animal the star of his flock. Heracles
took as little notice as people who live within sound of the sea do
of the sea, as young men, however susceptible, do of a lover
without money, as immoral sons do of their fathers, or (a typical
piece of Callimachean wit) Heracles himself did of music (he had

once beaten up his music teacher). The episode ends with a prayer:

> Welcome, hero of the club and the twelve prescribed Labors—
>   more still of your own choosing. (23)

The next episode followed from the theme of the killing of the ox. Heracles' son Hyllus was hungry. Thiodamas the Dryopian refused to help, so Heracles killed one of his plough-oxen. This is the explanation of his cult-title Ox-eater. According to the myth, war resulted, the Dryopes were defeated (Callimachus uses a vivid phrase about Heracles crushing them with a pestle), driven out and resettled, and the prince Hylas taken as a hostage. The story was characteristically told with a mixture of direct power and learned allusion.

The next story we know from other sources. Crotopus was king of Argos. The god Apollo fell in love with his daughter Psamathe, who bore him a son, Linus. Scared of her father's reactions, she gave the child away to be brought up by shepherds. The boy was killed by the king's hounds. The story came out and Crotopus condemned Psamathe to death. Now it was Apollo's turn to be angry, and he sent Poine (Punishment) to infect Argos with pestilence. The result was that the Delphic Oracle told the citizens to honor Psamathe and Linus; they established a Festival of Lambs and named one month Lambs' Month *(Arneios);* during the festival they avenged Linus by killing any strange dogs. Apollo was not fully appeased until Crotopus went into voluntary exile. The remains of Callimachus's treatment are tantalizingly fragmentary, and read rather like a poem by Ezra Pound:

>   Lambsmonth . . . . . .
>   Lambsfeast . . . .
>   it died.   (26, 1–3)

One exquisite couplet survives:

> Dear boy, lambs were your playfellows, lambs your companions,
>   your bedroom fold and field. (27)

It is easy to see the attraction of the complex aetiology for Callimachus.

Next came a lost story explaining why the statue of Artemis of Leucas had a mortar instead of a crown. Once the statue was crowned with gold, but pirates from Epirus raided Leucas, stole the crown, and in derision replaced it with a mortar. When the citizens tried to replace the golden crown it kept falling off, even when they nailed it on; so they consulted the oracle which told them to leave the mortar. The story is not known from any other source, and its presence here is attested only by the summary in a fairly recently discovered papyrus fragment[6].

The few remaining fragments of the first book are uncertain in scope and arrangement. But they contain one sparkling gem:

> An old man grows old more gracefully
> when young lads love him, and escort him like their own father
> hand in hand to his own door. (41)

IV   *The Second Book*

Nor do we know the arrangement of the second book. The most substantial fragment extends with some gaps to something like a hundred lines, and is a conversation with the Muses about the cities of Sicily and some of their traditions and curious practices—one of the subjects of this book. The descriptions are sometimes picturesque—

> I shall also speak of Camarina where curving Hipparis creeps
>   (43,42)

sometimes evocative—

> I know a city lying at the end of the river Gelas,
>   proud to belong to Lindus's line,
> and Cretan Minoa, where Cocalus's daughters gave Europa's son
>   a bath of boiling water. (43, 46-9)

This last refers to the legend that when the cunning Daedalus escaped airborne from Minos's autocratic power, Minos pursued him to Sicily where he had taken refuge with Cocalus, king of Camicus. Cocalus received him with Homeric courtesy, offering him a bath, but instructing his daughters, who were waiting upon their guest, to pour boiling water over him as he lay there. There is an odd piece of bird-lore about an otherwise unknown bird of prey, which we might call a snatch-hawk, whose presence lays a spell of black magic upon newly founded cities unless a counterspell is provided by a heron.

The account of the founding of Zancle is of particular interest. Zancle, the later Messene, near the straits which separate Sicily from Italy, is set on a curving bay, and means "sickle." This was mythologically linked with the sickle with which Cronos castrated his father Ouranos, the sky-god—an ancient cosmogonical myth—

> for the sickle with which he castrated his father is buried
> there in the earth. (43,70-1)

Another odd practice at Messene was that in offering sacrifice on official occasions the city-fathers did not invoke the founder by name, but said:

> "May our city's founder
> be gracious to attend our feast, bringing two or more:
> the victim's blood is copious!" (43,81-4)

This is explained by a quarrel between two joint founders, as a result of which Delphi decreed that neither should have the credit. Throughout this section the writing is interestingly varied. There is one remarkable piece of alliteration—

> No one who ever built any of these a wall
> fares forgotten to its festival. (43,54-5)

where the second line in Greek has two words beginning with *n* in the first half, and three beginning with *e* in the second, with assonance added: *nonumni nomimen erchet' ep' eilapinen.*

The only other episode in this book of which we can give any account was a double one, which must have been treated at length and with elaboration: indeed we must greatly regret losing it, for it offered Callimachus scope for skilled narrative and psychological observation. This combined two stories of human sacrifice. The first related to Busiris, king of Egypt. The land had been afflicted with nine years of drought in which the Nile floods had failed—an interesting parallel with the lean period recorded in Genesis. To allay the gods' anger Busiris began an annual sacrifice of a foreigner on the altar of Zeus (presumably Ammon), beginning with the Greek seer who recommended the practice. One of Heracles' adventures was his encounter with and killing of Busiris: the scene is depicted with magnificent comic verve in vase-painting[7]. Phalaris, dictator of Acragas in Sicily in the middle of the sixth century B.C. is said to have taken Busiris as a model, in a briefly alliterative line, packed (in the Greek) with scornful *ps*:

Phalaris followed his fashion. (45)

An inventor named Perillus served his purpose by devising a bull of bronze in which Phalaris secured his victims, lighting a fire underneath so that they were roasted alive, and their screams echoed within the bronze like the bull's bellowings: Callimachus calls it "death by bronze and fire" (46). Perillus was the first victim of his own monstrous device.

For the rest of the book we have only minute fragments. One refers to Zeus's three-hundred-year-long secret passion for Hera in the age of Cronos, before he himself was king of gods and men. Another must relate to an episode in the book. It consists of two words "Tammes' daughter's." Unfortunately we do not know which Tammes or which daughter. But the two words are characteristic of the poet: he refers to the girl by her patrilineage, not by her name, and he calls her father by the obscure name Tammes rather than the familiar Athamas. One Athamas founded Teos and had a daughter named Area, another came from Boeotia or Thessaly and had three daughters, Helle, Themisto, and Eurycleia. Helle is the most familiar of these, but that does not mean that she was Callimachus's theme.

Another reference describes Athens as "the only state to understand pity." Melos did not find her so in 416, when she sacked the island because its independent neutrality was an insult to her naval power.[8] It is notable that in Callimachus's day she had recovered that international reputation. The Altar of Pity had long stood in the city center there. Three or four centuries later, when it was proposed to introduce gladiatorial displays into Athens, the radical philosopher Demonax said that they would first have to destroy the Altar of Pity.

V   *The Third Book*

A cluster of fragments which must have come near the beginning of the next book relate to Molorchus, an elderly, not rich inhabitant of Cleonae. Heracles stayed with him. Molorchus, a man of piety, was about to offer sacrifice, but Heracles asked him to hold his hand for thirty days. If Heracles returned, the sacrifice should be to Zeus the Savior, if not, to Heracles himself. He then went off for his encounter with the Nemean lion

> unleashed by Zeus's testy wife
> to ravage Argos, sacred to her though it was, and to provide
> a hard task for Zeus's bastard boy. (55)

On the thirtieth day the hero returned triumphant, so the sacrifice was to Zeus the Savior. Heracles went off to Argos, and sent Molorchus a present of a mule. The treatment included the aetiology of the Nemean games:

> The prize they take won't be a horse or an ox-sized
> cauldron but a celery crown. (58)

A new discovery[9] seems to show that this was appropriately incorporated into an episode of some 200 lines celebrating a victory of queen Berenice in the chariot-race at Nemea. This may originally have stood on its own and been used as a proem to the third book balancing the episode of the Lock at the end of the fourth. The poet offered a grateful gift to Zeus and Nemea, a song to celebrate Berenice's victory. None of the other charioteers, even the leading ones, so much as warmed her driver's shoulders with their breath. Her horses ran as the wind; none saw their tracks. The foundation-myth of the Games then was inserted Pindarically into the epinician verse.

For the rest of the book the summaries give us the order. One episode showed the great poet Simonides speaking from the tomb, and telling of some of his achievements, his curious lore, and his invention of a system of mnemonics.[10] He recalls the episode when he was called out from a dinner party by two young men (later identified with Castor and Pollux) who thus saved him from the fate of the other diners when the roof fell in, and he complains about an otherwise unknown episode when a commander named Phoenix dismantled his tomb at Acragas, and built the stones into a defensive tower. This is typically described as "worse than moving Camarina," a lake which was disastrously drained against oracular advice, so that "Don't move Camarina" became proverbial.

There follows an account of the springs of Argos, derived no doubt from the local purveyor of Argive lore named Agias, whose work was edited in Callimachus's own day by an Alexandrian named Dercylus.[11]

> Lady Amymone, dear Physcadea,
> Hippe, Automate, ancient homes of nymphs, greetings.
> Flow, sparkling daughters of Pelasgus. (66,7-10)

Callimachus packs a great deal into those seemingly simple lines, for four images are closely blended. One is the springs themselves and the streams flowing from them; the second is the daughters of Danaus who discovered them, and gave their names to them; the third is the thought of the springs as homes of nymphs; the fourth is the nymphs themselves identified with the waters and appearing in the waters. Even the few lines which have survived show the expected interest in the rituals associated with the springs: the waters of Automate were, for example, used to cleanse a slave-girl after childbirth, the waters of Amymone to purify the girls chosen to weave the sacred robe for Hera, the great goddess of Argos.

Another episode long enough to permit more thorough evaluation of Callimachus's techniques is the story of Acontius and Cydippe, one of the loveliest of ancient love stories.[11] About a hundred lines survive in reasonable form. Callimachus took it from a fifth-century chronicler of Ceos named Xenomedes (75,54). Acontius, a handsome young man from Ceos who fluttered many hearts (68), saw Cydippe, a beautiful girl from Naxos, at the annual festival on the sacred island of Delos. The two were "brilliant stars" (67,8). He fell in love with her at first sight. The man who wounded others was smitten (70).

> No other girl who came near shaggy old Silenus's
> spring of water

looked more like the dawn than she, none who trod delicately
in dance to honor sleeping Ariede. (67,11-5)

Ariede is Ariadne, who was associated in myth with Naxos, where
Theseus abandoned her and Dionysus found her asleep. We do
not know Silenus's spring, but it must have been a Naxos
landmark. Callimachus evokes the girl's beauty with local color.
Acontius devised a stratagem.

Love—no other—was Acontius's teacher, when the lad
was burning for Cydippe's maiden beauty,
teaching him skill—the lad was free from guile—to win
that title for life. (67,1-4)

"That title" must be "Cydippe's mate". Acontius carved on a
quince the words "I swear by Artemis to marry Acontius," and, as
the girl entered Artemis's temple, dropped it in the path of her
attendant. The servant handed it to her mistress, who read the
inscription, naturally out loud, since virtually all reading in the
ancient world was out loud,[12] and thereby bound herself by the
oath taken in Artemis's name within Artemis's precincts.

They went their ways, the boy to a moody brooding, finding
any excuse for wandering off into the country (72), carving on
the trees "CYDIPPE—BEAUTIFUL" (73). Callimachus's account of this is a remarkable concatenation of double letters, as
the young man stammers out his love to the woodland.
Meantime, her father had other ideas about her marriage. Three
times he betrothed her; three times she fell ill. Callimachus
takes the opportunity to expound the marriage customs of Naxos
and to allude to ritual mysteries.

The girl was already asleep with a boy;
tradition demanded that a bride should spend the night before
marriage
with a boy of healthy, living parents.
Hera, it is said, once—stop, you low hound, you hound, my mind,
will you sing of unspeakable mysteries?
Lucky for you that you've never seen the Awesome Goddess's rites,
or you'd be spilling that story too.
It's dangerous if a polymath can't control his tongue;
he really is "a child with a knife". (75, 1-9)

It is a remarkable digression, remarkable in its violence and controlled vulgarity, remarkable in its assertion of his own values and the paradoxical application of a popular proverb. He returns to his story of the first planned marriage:

> At daybreak the oxen should have felt terror
>   seeing in the water the sharp knife—

it seems simple enough but it is highly allusive: the oxen are taken to a pool to be purified before sacrifice and see reflected in the water the man with the sacrificial knife behind them—

> but the previous afternoon a dreadful pallor gripped her, the disease
>   which we exorcise on to wild goats
> and falsely call Sacred. (75,10–4)

This is epilepsy. Callimachus has learned from the Hippocratics the folly of attributing it to the touch of a deity, even while so attributing it in his myth[13]: it is a beautiful "double take." Scapegoats might take disease away as well as sin, pollution in fact of any kind. Callimachus's compressed narrative makes another point. It was the previous afternoon that the girl was afflicted; yet she was ritually "bundled" with her boy-companion; her father must have dismissed her illness as psychosomatic, which it was, but not as he thought. But the oxen were to have had their purification in the early morning, and this was called off. So we get a whole picture of feverish activity by night between Callimachus's lines.

Three failures were too much for her father. He went to Delphi, and Apollo told him the story of the oath. The god addressed him chattily, as man to man, advertising Acontius with the persuasive advocacy of a marriage-broker.

> Ceyx, if you are willing to take my advice,
>   you'll now perform your daughter's vows.
> I tell you, in Acontius you won't be blending lead
>   with silver, but electrum with brilliant gold.
> You, his father-in-law, have Codrus as ancestor, your son-in-law
>   from Ceos has priests of Zeus Aristaeus,
> God of Moisture, whose task it is on the mountain peaks
>   to make fierce Maera gentle as she rises,
> and to plead with Zeus for the breeze which brings the quails
>   in masses to be caught in rope-snares. (75, 28–37)

Maera is the Dog Star, whose rising marked the dog days, a period of oppressive heat and danger of disease. Aristaeus was a local hero, Apollo's son, who saved Ceos from plague in the dog days by instituting a sacrifice to Zeus of Moisture. This led to his worship as Zeus Aristaeus. On the other side of the marriage Codrus was king of Athens; his son Promethus killed his brother and took refuge in Naxos. Callimachus makes his allusions precise.

Ceyx returned home and questioned the girl. The truth came out, and with it her health returned. The wedding was arranged.

> Acontius, I think on that night
>   when you unfastened her belt of virginity,
> the feet of Iphiclus skimming the corn-ears,
>   the wealth of Midas of Celaenae
> would not have attracted you—and so say all
>   who know the cruel god. (75, 44-9)

The cruel god is of course Love; Midas of Phrygia was proverbial for his golden touch, Iphiclus for speed such that he seemed to fly skimming the ground.

That, apart from the promise of famous descendants (the Acontiadae were a well-known family in Iulis), ends the story, but Callimachus rounds off the section with other stories of Ceos, naming its four cities and their founders (who are not otherwise recorded), and making something (in a reference which he anticipated in his new introduction to the poem) of the black magic of the Telchines which provoked the anger of the gods to annihilate the island—all but two women, Macelo and her daughter Dexithea, who married Minos of Crete, and gave birth to Acontius's line.

The rest of the third book comprises scraps only. An account of marriage customs in Elis might be said to pick up from the incidental account of the practice at Naxos. In Elis there was a practice that a bride was visited before marriage by an armed soldier. Callimachus's aetiological myth had to do with Heracles' massacring the citizens of Elis and sending his troops to sleep with the widows. This myth was also associated with the installation of the Olympic games. The next story told why the Ionian town of Isindus was excluded from the Panionian festival: one of its citizens murdered a guest of his, a serious offense at all

times in Greece. There is a gap in the summary at this point, and
we may assume another episode, but what we do not know. Next
follows the explanation why women in childbirth call upon a
virgin goddess, Artemis. Callimachus offered three accounts: one
is lost, even in the summary; the second is that it was a special
honor conferred by Ilithyia, the goddess of childbirth; the third
is that Artemis precociously helped her mother Leto in the birth
of her twin Apollo. Next came another love story. The cities of
Miletus and Myus were at war, till Phrygius, prince of Miletus,
fell in love with Pieria, princess of Myus: the rhetoric of love
proved stronger than any diplomacy. Phrygius addresses Pieria:

> "Your cheeks grew red with shyness, as if with rouge,
>   you spoke with your eyes. . . ." (80, 10-1)

The next story tells how Euthycles the Locrian, an Olympic
victor, was falsely accused of high treason. His statue was
dishonored. The city then succumbed to plague in punishment:

> So they were sent a harvest of horror
> by the Watcher-from-above, who cannot gaze
> with glad eyes on sinners. (85, 13-5)

They restored the statue to its honors and set up an altar. Finally,
we may reasonably fit into this book a fragment about Apollo's
statue on Delos.[14]

> "The Apollo of Delos?" "Yes." "Eighteen cubits high?"
>   "Yes, in my own name I swear it."
> "Formed of gold?" "Yes." "Nude?" "Yes,
>   just a belt around my middle."
> "God of Cynthus, why hold your bow in your left hand,
>   your lovely Graces in your right?"
>   " . . . . to check the violence of fools
>   . . . . I offer to the good." (114)

The answer is that the god is more disposed to bring blessings
than destruction.

VI *The Fourth Book*

We do not know how the fourth and last book started, as there is a gap in the summary account. It may be that here we should fit in the curious episode of the Mousetrap, though how it fitted in and what it was illustrating are hard to imagine. We know nothing of the central character, and nothing of the invention of the mousetrap. The scenario gives us an evening

> When the star which folds the flocks was ready to slacken
> the oxen's harness
> about the time of sunset (177, 5-6)

and an unknown man, whom we learn to be poor and plaguec with mice.

> Often they'd licked the lamp's rich oil,
> flicking it out with their tails, when the lid wasn't properly on.
> (177, 22-3)

They had eaten away his covering, his cloak, his knapsack in a single night. They would even dance on his head and stop him from sleeping. Now

> he heard a sound
> . . . as to the ears of a dappled deer
> comes a lion-cub's roar. He spoke quietly
> "Nuisances of neighbors, why
> have you come to gnaw at our home, certainly bringing no blessing?
> God made you a plague to our guests!" (177, 9-14)

There is delightful irony, both in the simile, and in his address to the mice. The man devised a mousetrap, using a flour mixture as bait.

> So he constructed two executioners,
> a trap and a catch expert in the long jump. (177, 32-3)

Again the description is ironical. The trap seems to have been of the type that springs on the mouse from a distance ("expert in the long jump"). There the fragment ends, frustratingly.

The summary resumes with the Delphic Daphnephoria. For most of this last book we have more, far more, of the summary than of the original, and may pass over the sections in rapid survey. This section dealt with the annual procession garlanded with bay leaves from Tempe to Delphi, originating in an act of Apollo after he killed the dragon. Next came a ritual from Abdera, a city on the fringes of the Greek world, which nonetheless produced Protagoras and Democritus, the purification of the arts through the driving out of a scapeman. Next an explanation of human sacrifice on the island of Tenedos in honor of Melicertes. His mother Ino (whom Callimachus calls by the dialectual form Byne) in a fit of madness drowned herself with her child—"moored to a single anchor," Callimachus boldly says, a child being commonly called an anchor, and a single anchor being insecure. The boy's body was washed ashore on Tenedos and a cult started. Human sacrifice leads to the sacrifice by the Etruscans of a heroic soldier named Theudotus, from the volcanic island of Lipara. There followed a story of seduction and punishment from Athens, the seducer being struck down and dragged around the city behind a horse, the girl, Limone or Limonis, being immured in a room with a horse. The story explains the existence of a place called "The Horse and the Girl."

"The Boastful Hunter" is an excellent cautionary tale. A hunter who had killed a boar hung the head on a tree in his own honor: it fell on him in his sleep and killed him. We do not know what later ritual ensued. Next followed an explanation of the so-called Pelasgian wall in Athens: Callimachus seems to have identified the Pelasgians with the Etruscans. Next came a story of Temese in south Italy. There they had the practice of offering a virgin in tribute. The legendary explanation of the practice went back to a companion of Odysseus named Lycus or Polites.[15] It was abolished in historical times by an Olympic boxer named Euthymus. Two accounts of statues of Hera, the great goddess of Samos, follow. The oldest statue was an unshaped block of wood, brought from Argos; this was the normal practice in early times, operating by serendipity on fortuitous appearances. The other statue, presumably the work of Scelmis, who is known only as the first artificer to fashion a statue of the goddess, had a vine and a lionskin. These were the symbols of Dionysus and Heracles, and were said to represent Hera's superiority to Zeus's bastard sons: it is interesting that the vine and lionskin seem to appear in association with the wooden statue on early coins of Samos.

Next follows a story of murder and tragic irony. Pasicles held high office in Ephesus. He was set upon as he left a dinner party. The assassins were frustrated by the darkness, but the noise as they passed Hera's temple led the priestess, who happened to be Pasicles' mother, to bring out a lamp, which led to her son's death. Hera provided the link with the previous episode, but we do not know what later practice ensued.

The next section is even more obscure. It gives an account of an inscription on a column in honor of Androgeos, son of Minos of Crete, and protector of the stern of ships. The story was somehow connected with the old Athenian harbor of Phalerum. Then comes an account of Oesydres of Thrace whose death was a bane to the island of Thasos: there was war in Thasos involving the Thracians in the seventh century, but we do not know more. Next comes perhaps, for the summary is in a very poor condition, something about a place in Thebes called the Syrma of Antigone. Antigone's brothers had killed each other in battle. One was accorded the right to cremation, the other cast out as a traitor. According to this version, Antigone succeeded in placing both bodies on the same pyre—and the flames of the fire split apart. Then follows a frustratingly uncertain story. "He tells that when the Peuceti were besieging Rome, a Roman named Gaius jumped down from the walls and killed their commander. He was wounded in the leg and later began to grumble about his limp. But when his mother commented adversely, he stopped worrying about it." She no doubt said, "My son, let your steps be a reminder of your patriotic courage." Who was this Gaius? We do not know him as such in Roman tradition. But if the mysterious Peuceti were the Etruscans, then Gaius with his limp might be none other than the famous Horatius Cocles, he who kept the bridge.

The last episode of *Aitia* as originally planned seems to have related to a story of the Argonauts. They left behind at Cyzicus the stone they were using as an anchor because it was too light: this stone was later dedicated to Athene. In this way Callimachus planned his work in ring form, beginning and ending with the Argonauts.

VII   *The Later Additions*

But this is not the end of the work as we have it. Berenice was granddaughter of Ptolemy I's queen Berenice I; her father was king of Cyrene. She had long been affianced to a Ptolemy, perhaps but not certainly Ptolemy III, but did not marry him till the death of Ptolemy II in 247 and Ptolemy III's accession. Almost immediately Antiochus II, king of Syria, whose wife was Ptolemy III's sister, was assassinated by the king's divorced wife Laodice. This was a *casus belli*, and Ptolemy embarked on the Third Syrian War or (as it was called in antiquity) Laodice's War. Berenice vowed to the gods a lock of her hair against her husband's safety. On his safe return, after his sister's death, and some contorted operations, military and diplomatic, the vow was fulfilled, and the lock offered in the shrine of Arsinoe II at Zephyrium near Canopus. The lock of hair mysteriously vanished. Conon, the court astronomer, was called in, and proceeded to identify it with a cluster of stars ringed by the Great Bear, Boötes, Virgo, and Leo:

> I adjoin the constellations of the Virgin and the fierce Lion,
> > next to Lycaon's child Callisto,
> as I move to my setting, leading the way for slow Boötes
> > who is reluctant to sink in Ocean's depths.
>
> (100, 65–8 from Catullus)

To celebrate this event Callimachus wrote a wittily clever court poem. A few years later when he came to revise *Aitia* for his collected works, he decided to incorporate this independent poem as a climactic episode. To this end he added a further sixteen lines, as the original witty conclusion did not fit the new setting.

For a long time our direct knowledge of Callimachus's poem consisted of a mere two or three isolated phrases. We had, however, the whole poem in a Latin translation by Catullus which he made during a period of acute depression after his brother's death, when he was unable to maintain his creative writing, but kept up his craftsmanship in this way. The sands of Egypt have in this century uncovered for us in the original Greek a consecutive passage of some twenty lines together with a few other crumbs from the table of time.[16] This is valuable in itself.

Equally important, it shows that Catullus for the most part kept close to his original, only occasionally diverging; indeed he has been highly skilled in conveying the flavor of the Greek, even to the alliteration, as when a line in the Greek beginning *Kupridos eis kolpous* (110, 56) becomes *et Veneris casto collocat in gremio.*

Callimachus's opening is characteristically direct, yet enigmatic:

> He scanned all the sections of the sky, observed
>   where the stars move. (110, 1)

We do not yet know who "he" is. Again characteristically, the poet passes, in Catullus's version, to a combination of vivid description and mythological allusion:

> how the flaming glory of the speeding sun is blotted out,
>   how at regular seasons constellations vanish,
> how Trioditis is secretly banished to the rocky cave of Latmos,
>   summoned from her circuit in the air by love's delights.
>   (110, 3–6)

Trioditis (Latin Trivia) is Hecate, who was worshipped at road junctions: but she has different existences, Artemis on earth, Selene, the moon, in the sky. Selene fell in love with a young shepherd of Latmos, Endymion. Now we find the answer to the enigma.

> That same Conon saw me too in the air, Berenice's lock,
>   whom she dedicated to all the gods. (110, 7–8)

So we have the solution to a second riddle: the speaker is the lock of hair. The occasion was the departure of the newly married king on campaign,

> carrying the delightful trophies of warfare by night
>   fought over the spoils of virginity. (110, 13–4)

The metaphor, though trite, is effective.

A curious passage follows. Callimachus says that the tears of young brides are insincere. It is not clear whether he is referring to the tears shed at the thought of approaching marriage, or the tears shed in the first experience of marriage. Either way it is an odd thing to say. His point is that the intensity of Berenice's grief at her husband's departure for war made all other grief seem faked. He goes on to an even stranger sentiment: it was not the empty bed that grieved her so much as parting from a brother. This is an allusion to the Ptolemaic practice of brother-sister marriage (though Berenice was not literally Ptolemy's sister), but it is also a piece of folklore found in Herodotus, and in Sophocles' *Antigone,* and incidentally in traditional West African society, that you can get another wife or husband more easily than another brother or sister. The Lock goes on to speak of the courage she had shown in the past, which at that moment failed her, to speak with down-to-earth candor:

> What god's power transformed you? Is it that lovers
>   can't bear to be far from the body they love? (110,31-2)

At this point she made her vow. It didn't take Ptolemy long, says the Lock with pardonable exaggeration, to capture Asia and add it to the dominion of Egypt.

> I am the due requital of this to the company of the gods.
>   With a present gift I fulfill your past promise. (110, 37-8)

Then comes the famous whimsical couplet:

> I did not want to leave your head, my queen:
>   by your head, by your life, I swear it. (110,39-40)

Catullus made that first line *invita, o regina, tuo de vertice cessi,* a line which Vergil, with "shore" for "head," surprisingly borrowed to put into the mouth of Aeneas when he met Dido in the underworld. There follows a new conceit, full of enigmatic allusion. The Lock protests that it could not withstand the power of steel (in the knife which cut it off):

> Even the great mountain was tumbled down, the tallest
>   which Theia's bright son crosses,
> the obelisk of your mother Arsinoe, and the Persian warships
>   sailed through the middle of Athos. (110, 43-6)

Theia's descendant is Boreas, the North Wind. Athos is the great mountain in the north of Greece, later the retreat of monastic communities: we do not know why it was called Arsinoe's obelisk (more literally "ox-piercer"). The Persians under Xerxes cut a canal, not of course through the mountain, but through the isthmus joining it to the mainland. Now a fresh allusion, to a legendary tribe of smiths:

> What can we locks of hair do, when such mountains succumb
>> to steel? Damn the whole tribe of Chalybes,
> who first brought from underground that abominable growth
>> and taught men to use hammers! (110, 47-50)

There is a conceit in the thought of iron as a vegetable.

Now Callimachus can place all his mythological learning and ingenuity at the service of his imagination.

> My sister locks missed one when I was first cut off.
>> Swiftly black Memnon's brother,
> the gentle breeze, the mount of Locrian Arsinoe with her violet girdle,
>> sped with whirling wings,
> seized me with his breath, carried me through the rains of the lower air,
>> set me in Cypris's lap. (110, 51-6)

Memnon's brother is Zephyrus, the West Wind. The deified Arsinoe was worshipped as Arsinoe Aphrodite (Cypris) at Zephyrium. There is a whole complex of interwoven allusions: yet the description is fresh, vivid, and picturesque. The Lock goes on to describe how he was settled in the sky, and ends with a little flattery of the queen, and a final witty conclusion:

> These honors bring me less joy than the pain I feel
>> that I shall never again touch that head,
> from which, while I was still unwedded, I drank many simple
>> perfumes, but never enjoyed the myrrh which a wife may use.
>>>> (110, 75-8)

Here Callimachus ended his original free-standing poem. It was suave, witty, courtierly: it fitted the mood of relaxation and relief that must have filled the court in the weeks after Ptolemy's victorious return. When he came to incorporate the poem in *Aitia* he added an *aition*, linking his contemporary myth with a contemporary marriage-rite:

> Now you girls, when the torch with the light you long for has
> united you,
>   don't yield your bodies to your loving husbands,
> unfastening your clothes and baring your breasts, until
>   the onyx jar offers me the gifts I delight in,
> the onyx that's yours while your bedroom is chaste, your
> vows faithful.
>   If any is unchaste and adulterous,
> may her offerings be cursed, soaked up by the light dust,
> ·unfulfilled.
>   I want no gifts from the worthless. (110, 79–86)

Callimachus, we must not forget, was a poet with ethical as well
as literary values. At the end he returns to his wit. The Lock asks
the queen to offer him perfumes in plenty—"I am of you"—and
concludes, envisaging the sky without his own constellation:

> Why do the stars hold me here? Set me on the queen's head again,
>   and let Orion blaze next to Aquarius. (110, 93–4)

It is a witty conclusion to a poem of unusual point. This self-
contained episode was of course the remote ancestor of a very
differently witty poem, Alexander Pope's *The Rape of the Lock*.

To this final episode in the revised version Callimachus
offered a brief epilogue. The fragments of this raise unanswered
questions. The poet invoked Zeus and some goddess, but
whether Aphrodite, or Cyrene, or the Muse Calliope remains
unclear. A reference to the Graces helps to place the whole
poem in ring form: so, still more effectively, does the allusion to
Hesiod:

> . . . as he pastured his flocks of sheep
> by the high-mettled horse's hoofprint the Muses shared stories
> with him. (112, 5–6)

He offers a prayer for the royal house, and then in a final
line—

> I will pass to the Muses' prosaic measure (112,9)—

leads his reader on to the *Iambi*.

VIII *Unplaced Fragments*

We have some passages belonging to *Aitia* which we cannot attribute with certainty to any one book. They add something to our appreciation of Callimachus's polymathy. One for example is the story of a couple, apparently named Onnes and Tottes. The fragment is obscure, and the figures are not known from any other source. They evidently have something to do with forging and the work of the smith. It is a plausible guess, but no more, that they may be associated with the Cabeiri, mysterious, pre-Hellenic powers worshipped on the coast of Asia Minor and portrayed with hammers: they are often said to be the gods of the Samothracian Mysteries, but that is due to a false equation by Herodotus.

A substantial fragment has to do with the cult of Peleus on the small island of Icos. It is unusual in being set in a reminiscent context. Callimachus was the guest of an Athenian named Pollis who had settled in Alexandria, but was careful to keep the Athenian festivals.

He did not miss the dawn of Jar-opening or the time when Orestes's
    Pitchers mark a white day for slaves. (178, 1-2)

The present dinner party was at the time of the Aiora. Among the guests was a businessman from Icos, named Theugenes. Callimachus found himself next to Theugenes.

I shared a couch with him,
    not deliberately, but the Homeric saw stands—
    God always brings like to like. (178, 8-10)

So Callimachus characteristically brings in a traditional saying. They found common ground in abhorring greedy drinking. Callimachus goes on to his neighbor sententiously:

"It's a true saying: wine demands its share of water—
    and its share of talk as well.
Talk is not passed around and served in ladles." (178, 15-17)

So he brings together a familiar cliché and an epigram of his own.

He speaks to his new friend in a way not very complimentary to
the dinner party, "Let us toss talk in to sweeten a sour drink."
Then he begins to fire questions.

> "Why does your country traditionally worship Peleus, king
> of the Myrmidons? How does Icos fit in with Thessaly?"
> (178, 73-4)

We lack the answers, but it is an endearing picture of the poet
and scholar making quick friends with a stranger, and losing no
chance to add to his store of knowledge. It is also a refreshingly
original treatment of a *symposion*.

The third unplaced theme has to do with the elusive
Hyperboreans, an idealized, just, vegetarian, long-lived, noble,
pious, musical, mythical tribe, living "beyond the North Wind,"
who were somehow associated with Apollo, and offered him
sacrifice of donkeys. The only passage which makes sense is
typical of the poet's allusive learning:

> . . . the sons of the Hyperboreans
> send from the Rhipaean range, where Phoebus
>   delights in the generous sacrifice of asses.
> The Pelasgian Ellopians were the first of the Greeks
>   to take these from Arimaspian bearers.
> From there the attendants on Zeus Naios, with feet unwashed,
>   send them
>   to the cities and hills of Malis. (186, 8-14)

The Rhipaean range lies up near the Danube. Ellopia, Pelasgian
Ellopia, is near Dodona, and "Pelasgian" emphasizes the
antiquity of the connection. The Arimaspians are neighbors of
the Hyperboreans; Herodotus (4,13) calls them one-eyed and
says that they collect gold from griffins. Zeus Naios is god of
Dodona, and his priests, the Selloi, were characterized by their
unwashed feet. Malis is an area of eastern Greece.

IX *Summary*

The structure of *Aitia* eludes us: the old hypothesis that each
book had a consistent theme does not hold water. The poem
attracted by variety rather than by logical consistency. The
poet's sources were various. He places his episodes in different

settings. One may be a revelation by one of the Muses, another an imagined conversation with the hero of the story, another an actual conversation with a casual acquaintance. The poet's own voice continually breaks through, in question or exclamation or aside to the reader. Emile Cahen characterized it neatly: "a many-sided and entertaining book of rather formal charm."[17] H. J. Rose compared *Aitia* with Edgar Allan Poe's work, lacking the latter's flashes of morbid genius.[18] T. B. L. Webster called it "a great outpouring of scholarship," found it difficult to evaluate how far individual poems came alive because of their fragmentary nature and because tastes have changed, but approved in the longer passages the elegance, humor, learning, and variety which we expect from the poet.[19]

CHAPTER 3

Iambi

I *Iambic Poetry*

THE Greeks regarded the iambic meter (alternating short and long syllables; strictly using as unit either ♪♪♩ or ♩♩♪) as approximating to natural speech rhythms. They used it for dialogue in drama, in contrast with the lyric effusions of the chorus: classical Greek had a pitch-accent, so that there remained a singsong or chanted effect, but the words were definitely spoken, not set to a melody. Iambics were used for a more prosaic type of poetry—fables, for instance, or proverbial wisdom. One variety of the iambic meter inverted the rhythm at the end of each line, creating a stumbling effect, a harshness. This was called the scazon (limping), choliambic (lame iambic), or Hipponacteon (after Hipponax of Ephesus, its first great exponent). It was used for satirical lampoons. In common parlance the word *iambic* came to be associated with such lampoons: a fragment of the Roman poet Catullus runs "But you won't escape my iambics" but the iambic meters were always more varied and put to more varied uses.

The three great early exponents of the iambic meter were Archilochus, Semonides, and Hipponax. Archilochus was the greatest, the putative inventor of the genre, a towering original genius, who wrote in a variety of meters, and used each for a variety of usually mordant purposes:

> I do not want the possessions of golden Gyges,
> I am not jealous of him, I don't aspire to
> the acts of the gods, have no desire to be a dictator.
> All this is far from my eyes.

Semonides is best known for a long misogynous poem, comparing women with animals; from the other fragments he seems to have specialized in animal-comparisons. But Hipponax was the most vigorous and downright of them all. *The Suda* tells us that he was a political exile. He complained about the blindness of the god of wealth, who never visited him, and prayed to Hermes for some lined shoes and an overcoat to stop his teeth from chattering. He seems to have invented the Hipponacteon, though this is also attributed to a poet named Ananius, author of a poem on gastronomy. Certainly Hipponax made it his own, and used it to pursue a sculptor named Bupalus—to suicide, later legend averred. He was coarse and candid: one fragment is a treasure for collectors of erotica. But he was capable of laughing at himself.

The great flurry of iambic activity, drama apart, thus belonged to the sixth century. We know of one or two fifth-century writers, Hermippus the one-eyed (who prosecuted Pericles' mistress Aspasia and lampooned the demagogue Hyperbolus) and Scythinus of Teos. In the next century we know even fewer, though perhaps here is to be dated the shadowy figure of Chares, who wrote gnomic verses, taking off from some of Euripides' more epigrammatic lines.

It seems possible then that Callimachus, in using the iambic meter for nondramatic purposes, and especially for lampoons, was innovatory rather than working within a living tradition. He himself implies as much in his initial appeal to Hipponax: he claims to be Hipponax *redivivus*. But this is not an antiquarian revival. It is Callimachus's realization that the traditions of the past can be used to speak directly to the present, and he so uses them. They are not a slight experiment. They are thirteen poems and we know that they constituted a complete book, so that we can reasonably assume that the original totaled about 1000 lines. The fourth poem contained more than 100 lines; the others of which substantial fragments remain exceeded 50 lines; we may also assume that none exceeded 150 lines and the majority were between 50 and 100. It was a considerable achievement. Callimachus made the iambics part of his poetic self.

Other choliambics survive from the third century, notably from Phoenix of Colophon.[1] The meter seems to have fitted the Cynic mood and temper particularly well. More likely these survivals followed Callimachus's usage rather than the other way around.

II   *The Introductory Poem*

It is possible that the first poem was written after the others: it was not uncommon to add a prefatory poem later to a collection. But there is no clear internal evidence of the date of writing. Euhemerus is described as "old" but as we do not know his dates this hardly helps. There is reference to a temple of Sarapis, but scholars disagree about the date of this. Other judgments are subjective; C. M. Dawson writes of the "tone of assured pre-eminence and self-confidence with which the poet speaks"; to prove a different case one might suggest "youthful bumptious-ness". The case is not proven, but it is not disproved either. The core of the poem consisted of a story of a certain Amphalces from Arcadia who was sent by his father to award a solid gold cup to the wisest man in the world. This would plainly be one of the Seven Sages, but each in turn, starting with Thales, disclaimed it and when it came back to Thales, he dedicated it to the Protector of Miletus. Callimachus got this story from a Milesian writer named Leandrios;[2] what matters is the use to which he put it.

The meter he chose was the scazon or limping iambic, a safe indication of satirical intent. The dialect is a literary Ionic.

The theme is given in the summary. The satire is directed against jealously quarreling scholars. Callimachus imagines Hipponax, the great early exponent of mordant satire, risen from the dead, and summoning the scholars to a temple of the god Sarapis. This is important; Bryn Rees suggests that the scholar-poets are surrounded by statues of the learned from the past.[3] Callimachus's satire begins with admirable directness:

> Listen to Hipponax. I have come from
> the place where they sell oxen one a penny.
> Satire's my weapon, and its warsong isn't
> against Bupalus. (191, 1–4)

Goods are bargain-price in the land of the dead. Bupalus was one of the victims of the historic Hipponax. But his present victims will be of the present. The scholars come in crowds, as academics will to a distinguished visiting lecturer:

By Apollo, the men are swarming
like wasps from the ground, flies on a goatherd,
Delphians from a sacrifice. By Hecate, what a number! (191, 20-2)

The Delphians notoriously tried to grab for themselves the
sacrificial meat: Aesop told them off for it. There follows a
vividly obscure couple of lines:

Old Baldie will waste his lung-power
blowing to avoid loss of his patched cloak.

We do not know what that means; perhaps it refers to a Cynic
philosopher. Hipponax begins his moral story with realistic
jerkiness:

A man of Arcadia—it won't be long in the telling—
named Bathycles—don't turn up your nose, my good fellow:
I haven't time to waste! I'm in for a spin to the center
of hell. Oh dear!—was one of the blessed
of the past, had everything gods or humans
need to mark days as red-letter. (191, 32-7)

(The Greeks called them "white" days, marked with a white
pebble.) We have a picture of the old man, crippled with
arthritis, propping himself up on his elbow as if at a drinking
party, and addressing his sons—his anchors, he calls them. Then
after a gap in our text, we find Amphalces going in search of
Thales, who is credited with plotting the stars of the Little Bear,
"which Phoenicians use for sailing": like much of the poet's
scholarship, this is not quite gratuitous. The Arcadians were
believed to be a primeval people, and Callimachus calls the boy
Prelunar, or, as we would say, Antediluvian.

That Antediluvian by a stroke of fortune
found the old man in the temple of Didyma scratching
the dust with a stick and drawing the figure
which Euphorbus of Phrygia discovered,
the first person to draw unsymmetrical triangles
and add a circle, and to teach men to abstain
from living creatures. (191, 56-62)

Thales was a distinguished mathematician; he is represented as a follower of Pythagoras (who believed himself to be a reincarnation of Euphorbus, a character in the Trojan War). We know of Pythagoras's interest in right-angled triangles, and the reference, though not wholly clear, seems to refer to the fact that a triangle inscribed within a semicircle with a diameter as base will always be right-angled. It is a typical and not unattractive piece of Callimachean learning. The boy explains his errand. Thales sends him on to Bias. The rest of the poem is fragmentary, but "the prize drifted back to Thales," and Callimachus shows his metrical ingenuity by transcribing into scazons the inscription with which he dedicated it.

What happened after Hipponax had told his story is uncertain. He drew the moral that the scholars should be modest and not quarrelsome. Two vigorous fragments perhaps describe the behavior of scholars to one another.

> If anyone sees him he'll shout "He's an Alcmaeon!"
> "Run away from him!" he'll say. "Away! he's dangerous."
> (191, 78-9)

Alcmaeon was a proverbial madman; especially familiar to the Greeks because of his presentation in a lost play by Euripides. The point may be inverted: this is how they treat a man of generous impulse. Again:

> Behind there's a Corycian, mouth open,
> tongue curling like a dog drinking.
> (191, 82-3)

The Corycians were pirates, who spied on others, and used what they overheard to foster their purposes of plunder. "Any busybody, or anyone who tries to eavesdrop on people engaged in private conversation is called a Corycian" says Strabo. (14, 644). Callimachus has more point: here is one scholar spying on others in order to steal their results. The picture of academic life is still relevant. Hipponax completed his sermon and returned to the world of the dead.

III   *The Core-poems*

The second poem, also in scazons and literary Ionic, takes off from Aesop.[4] Originally all the animals, including men, had a common language.

> Once upon a time, the fishes,
> birds, and four-footed creatures,
> could talk like Prometheus's clay product. (192, 1-3)

Their prosperity made them insolent and they began to challenge Zeus's dispensations, the swan voicing a demand for immortality and the fox complaining of the injustice that the snake in sloughing its skin could renew its youth. Zeus punished their rebellion by severing them from speech and giving them many tongues, transferring their loquacity to man. Callimachus makes this an occasion for irony, as he inverts the fox's complaint:

> Zeus is just, but his ruling was unjust
> when he severed speech from animals,
> directing it to creatures in this defective—
> as if we hadn't plenty to share with others!—
> humans. (192, 6-10)

We come to the point of the satire. Callimachus does not make anything of the different languages of mankind. He addresses his gall to individuals; that we know nothing about them hardly lessens the power.

> A dog's bark—that's Eudemus.
> A donkey's bray—Philton. A parrot's squawk—politicians.
> The tragedians have the voice of the inhabitants
> of ocean. All human beings
> have grown into long-winded gasbags
> through this, my dear Andronicus. (192, 10-5)

The third poem, also in the same meter and dialect, is of slight interest, and only a small intelligible fragment survives. The poem started from a generalized statement, following Hesiod, of the inferiority of the present to the past.

> Lord Apollo, if only I'd lived before my own day,
> when honor was paid to you and the dear Muses. (193, 1-2)

In his day, values are materialistic. We soon come to the point of the complaint. One Euthydemus, of whom we know nothing except his physical attraction, has given up Callimachus for a rich rival, Callimachus has chosen the wrong divinities to serve:

> . . . for me it would have proved better
> . . . to toss my hair in Cybele's honor
> to the sound of Phrygian flute, or with cloak dragging
> to mourn for the goddess's man, Adonis,
> poor Adonis. But I'm a fool. The Muses
> were my object. I must eat the bread I kneaded. (193, 34-9)

He may grumble that the Muses don't grant wealth, but he doesn't disown them.

We have rather more of the fourth poem, an amusing little fable, still in the same meter and dialect. According to the summary, Callimachus and a rival poet were in an argument when a man named Simos whom Callimachus treats as a climber and an upstart, and evidently called a "Thracian" (an innuendo about paederasty), tried to intervene. Callimachus then embarked on the story of the laurel and the olive. The intelligible fragments start with the claims of the laurel, who pokes fun at her rival's parti-colored leaves:

> Your left side is white as a watersnake's belly,
> the other, through exposure to the sun, roasted. (194, 22-3)

She makes her claims; she's by every doorway, carried by every prophet or priest:

> the Pythia sits on laurel,
> sings of laurel, lies on laurel . . .
> I'm always at dinners, always at Delphic
> dances, I'm presented to victors. (194, 26-7, 32-3)

"Ridiculous olive" she keeps calling her rival, and points to the olive's connection with cremation and burial.

The olive gives as good as she receives; Callimachus uses a legal metaphor; she dismisses the other's case:

> Beautiful! My own greatest beauty
> came at the end of your swan song. (194, 46–7)

She is proud of escorting the dead. Olive crowns were prizes at
the Olympic games, which ranked above the Pythian games,
which used laurel. At this point Callimachus introduces a stock
rhetorical device. To avoid boastfulness he lets the olive quote a
third party, two birds chattering in the trees. Further, he uses
another rhetorical device, for the two birds in question-and-
answer form set the pros and cons as firmly as any sophistic
handbook.

> "Who produced the laurel?" "Earth and . . .
> like the oak, galingale, pine and holm-oak."
> "Who produced the olive?" "Pallas long ago
> when she fought her seaweed-housed adversary
> for Attica, and a snake-tailed judge gave the verdict."
>   (194, 64–8)

This is an allusion to the rivalry between Poseidon and Athene
for Attica. Poseidon, in horse form, stamped his hoof and
produced a spring; Athene's gift was the olive; the snake-tailed
judge was the legendary king Cecrops. The metaphor of the
contest now changes to wrestling.

> "One fall against the laurel. Which of the immortals
> cherished the olive, which the laurel?"
> "Apollo the laurel, Pallas her own invention."
> "A tie: no distinction between deities.
> What's the laurel's fruit? for what is it useful?"
> "Don't use it for food, drink, or ointment.
> The olive's fruit is staple fare for down-and-outs
> (they call it olivecake), it's used for anointing,
> olive juice was even downed by Theseus."
> "I award a second fall against the laurel.
> Which has its leaves used in supplication?"
> "The olive." "Three falls against the laurel."
> "Oh dear! how they go on, those creatures!" (194, 69–81)

We can see that Callimachus's poem has three dimensions. Its
primary purpose is to put down Simos; it gives him a chance to
display his poetical and rhetorical skill in telling a good story. But
it is also a defense of his own poetry. By implication he allows his

rival poetic inspiration. But that is not enough. Callimachus is claiming for his own verse grace and utility; it gives spiritual nurture to those who take it, and it offers delight as well.

The poem proceeds to its overt point. A briar tries to horn in on the conversation, and is rejected by the laurel, who glares like a bull and says

> "You pestilential nuisance,
> d'you think you're one of us? Don't do
> that to me, Zeus! Your very closeness chokes me." (194, 102–4)

At this point our text fades out. It was evidently an important poem to Callimachus. At some points the text recalls his *Hecale,* but we cannot be certain whether he is alluding to it as a past achievement, or building up to it.

The fifth poem is in a different meter, though still one used by Hipponax; the scazons alternate with shorter iambic lines. It is directed to an elementary teacher, and Callimachus whimsically begins with a couple of the proverbial saws that formed his stock in trade.

> My friend—there's "sanctity in advice"—
> "listen to words from the heart."
> Fortune has saddled you with the ABC. . . . (195, 1–3)

The teacher has been abusing his charges sexually. The poet warns him allusively; the passage was taken as a classic example of *allegoria,* euphemistic writing which says one thing and means another:

> You've lit a fire, but it hasn't yet burst out
>   in flaring flame;
> it's still, stirring among the ashes.
>   Put it to sleep. Control
> the wild horses' charging. No second lap, or
>   they'll smash up your car
> at the turn, tipping you topsy-turvy. (195, 23–9)

The next two poems are different. They are in literary Doric with some variations, and the meter alternates straightforward iambics with shorter ithyphallics (a trochaic rhythm, which thus reverses the direction of the previous line). They are not aggressive or satirical. The sixth is a *propempticon,* a poem of good wishes for a journey. The friend is going to Olympia to see Phidias's statue of Zeus, which centuries later Quintilian was to declare added something to revealed religion and which was to occasion one of Dio of Prusa's most powerful and eloquent addresses. Callimachus used the occasion for a tour-de-force in which he described the statue, its dimensions and accoutrements, in impeccable verse, of which little survives.

Next comes an *aition,* a poem explaining why at Aenus in Thrace Hermes was called the "Passed-around" *(Perpheraios).* We have only the characteristic opening.

> I'm Hermes the Passed-around, the god of Aenus,
>   work of the Phocian who fled
> the war, but built the horse, a by-product.
>   A clever fellow
> . . . his adze. . . . (197, 1–5)

This skillful shirker was Epeus. The by-product statue of Hermes was washed away in a flood, and salvaged by some fishermen at Aenus. They tried unsuccessfully to chop it up for firewood, then to burn it. Failing, they threw it back. Again they caught it in their nets, and now offered it reverence as their first fruits, passing the image from hand to hand, and building it a shrine.

Callimachus was interested in writing epinician poems in honor of athletic victors in simple meters instead of the complex constructions favored by Pindar, Simonides, and Bacchylides in the past; we have other examples in elegiacs. The eighth poem was of this kind: it was probably in straight iambics, though little enough survives. We know that the poem was for Polycles of Aegina who won the jar race in a local festival at home: this consisted in running to a jar full of water, picking it up, and running back with it. Tradition favored incorporating a myth in the congratulatory ode and Callimachus's interest in *aitia* led him to an explanatory myth. The Argonauts landed on Aegina, the wind was favorable, and to restock the ship speedily with water they raced one another.[5] Scarcely any of Callimachus's poem is left:

Once upon a time, with a gentle southern breeze, the *Argo* (198) but it is possible that we should include here a couple of lines in which the poet compares himself with the great Simonides:

> . . . I do not train my Muse to be
> a wage-slave, like Hylichus's son from Ceos. (222)

Another *aition* is found in the ninth poem. A young man in love sees an ithyphallic statue of Hermes:

> Hermes of the Long Beard, why does your penis point
> to your beard and not your feet? (199)

Is it because the god too has seen the handsome Philetadas? The poem was evidently a dialogue between the young man and the god, who rebuked him roundly. His own ithyphallic posture was due to a mystic cause (we do not know exactly what it was), Etruscan in origin. The Greeks identified the Etruscans with the Pelasgians, and other sources suggest that ithyphallic Hermes was of Pelasgian origin.[6] Further, the god went on, his interlocutor was up to no good with Philetadas, and had better lay off him. We should suppose an actual situation, and may guess that Callimachus himself had interest in Philetadas, and was warning off a rival.

The tenth poem reverts to the Ionic dialect, and is also in iambic trimeters. It also is aetiological, but with no obvious topicality. It explains the sacrifice of a boar to Aphrodite at Aspendus in terms of promise made on a hunting expedition. This might make a tolerable poem of itself, but Callimachus insists on a greater measure of complexity and adds a second *aition* to explain the fact that Artemis Colaenis on Euboea did not, like most deities, demand perfection from her sacrificial animals.

> Agamemnon (the story has it) dedicated the image,
> and tailless and one-eyed animals are offered to it. (200B)

Apparently Agamemnon offered a defective *(colos)* ram in the original sacrifice, and this is used as an explanation of cult and cult-title alike.

Next, though only a single line survives, comes a poem in a very rare meter, iambic, but with only five feet to the line instead of the regular six (2½ double feet instead of a trimeter). The poem was an explanation of a proverbial saying, seemingly often misquoted, as Callimachus is at pains to show. "The goods of Connidas are anyone's game." Connidas made his money in the white-slave business. He used to say that he would divide his riches between Aphrodite and his friends, but when he died his will read "The goods of Connidas are anyone's game." When this came to the ear of the people of Selinus in Sicily where he lived, they left the theater *en masse* and looted his estate. We can be fairly certain that the poet's source was a *Sicilian Historian,* Timaeus of Tauromenium.[7] Callimachus, whose sense of the appropriate seldom failed him, used Doric for this poem. He seems to have begun with Connidas speaking from the tomb, a device used widely in poetic epitaphs, and swearing (again appropriately) by his local river Hypsas. But we do not know how he developed the theme.

With many of these poems we have been clutching at straws, but the twelfth, one of the most interesting, offers more substance. The rhythm is trochaic, the dialect Ionic. The poem is a birthday gift for the seventh-day naming ceremony of Callimachus's friend Leon's newborn daughter; it must therefore have been written in the week between the birth and the ceremony. The poet begins by invoking Artemis as goddess of childbirth, and praying for her blessing on Leon's home. He calls also on the Fates to grant his request, and the Muse to inspire the verse he will offer. He then tells the myth of Hebe's birth. All the gods and goddesses joined in friendly rivalry to bring her gifts. Zeus came with worthy offerings, Athene produced skillfully made toys, as did Poseidon (who is described as "the watcher at Apis's neck"; Apis being a legendary king of Argos, who gave his name to the Peloponnese as Apia, the neck being the isthmus of Corinth, sacred to the sea-god). Apollo thought differently:

> I shall prepare a different gift.
> Phoebus, you must try your artistry,
> finer than Hephaestus's finest.
> Indian dogs can carry gold, —

we do not know them, but they were evidently a kind of insect —

> ants, from earth's depths on their wings.
> Gold is often found in a house of

crime, dishonoring ancient ways.
Men will kick away, rejecting
Zeus and Laws and Justice's claims,
praising gold, that sinful glory.
Time as it marches on will dim
Pallas's and the others' gifts,
carved with all their fine precision.
Mine's the noblest gift to the girl, and
while the hair on my cheeks is smooth
while wolves love to prey on kids. . . ." (202, 55-70)

The text breaks off, but we can see that Callimachus is making claims about the immortality of poetry and the consequent immortality conferred by poetry, as surely as Shakespeare in his lines:

So long as men can breathe, or eye can see,
So long lives this, and this gives life to thee.

It expresses his own judgment of value. More, it is a proud assertion that his gift to Leon's daughter is the most valuable she will receive. That gift too has suffered the ravages of time — but it has in fact survived, and the little girl, yet unnamed, is still with us.

IV   *The Concluding Poem*

With the last poem of this book Callimachus returns to a direct statement of his poetic values and an attack on his critics, and uses the scazon and the Ionic dialect. His critics had complained that he put his hand to too many things: he did not specialize. It is a common enough complaint today whether on the literary or academic scene, and Callimachus anyway had a foot in both those camps. We do not know who the critics were: they include the Telchines of the opening of *Aitia*. We know what Callimachus's answer was. He claimed as his justification the example of the popular fifth-century poet, Ion of Chios, best known as a tragedian, but writer also of comedies, dithyrambs, lyrics, poems, hymns, encomia, epigrams, drinking songs as well as prose compositions.[8] He also appealed to the practice of craftsmen who make a variety of products. Unfortunately, although quite a substantial part of the poem is extant, the text is

uncertain, difficult to read, and obscure when read. Callimachus
began with an invocation to the Muses and Apollo. A reference to
the early poet Mimnermus has no clear context. Then follows:

> not consorting with Ionians,
> not visiting Ephesus with its many peoples,
> Ephesus from which budding poets
> learn to produce skillful scazons.

Hipponax came from Ephesus.

> But when there's inspiration for heart or stomach,
> whether it's traditional or unfamiliar,
> it's woven in and they speak . . .
> Ionic, Doric, or a mixture.
> How far will you venture? Your friends will have a straitjacket
> and if they've any sense, pour an offering to Sanity,
> seeing that you don't touch Sanity with a fingernail.
>   (203, 11-21)

It is hard to know what this means, or even who is speaking.
Perhaps this is the voice of the critics. The next clear fragment is
pellucid:

> "You write elegies—you epics—
> you've the gift of tragedy from heaven."
> I don't believe anyone said that. (203, 31-3)

Callimachus is denying specialist inspiration. The next is also
pellucid—

> As it is you burble absolute rubbish (203, 40)—

though whether it is addressed by Callimachus to his critics or
the critics to Callimachus is anyone's guess. But surely it is
Callimachus with his own voice who complains that

> one poet is roused against another poet
> to the point of violence. (203, 52-3)

There is a vivid picture of women shooting past the poet, nervous
of their reputations. Then, in a characteristically relevant simile
combined with a metaphor,

> That's why it's scraps, not rich fare that
> each scrapes off with his finger-tips,
> just as with the olive tree, Leto's relief. (203, 60-2)

The sacred olive-tree on Delos, where Leto gave birth to Apollo
and Artemis, was the prey for souvenir-hunters who scraped off
tiny pieces of bark. Callimachus then appears to throw back in
the face of his critics the charges they have leveled at him.

> So . . . I do not sing
> as a visitor to Ephesus, consorting with Ionians,
> Ephesus from which budding poets
> learn to produce skillful scazons. (203, 63-6)

One or two odd fragments whose location is not specified may
belong here, particularly a reference to "the tragic muse with its
hollow voice" (215). But that is all.

It is frustrating, as this was evidently a major statement of
poetic intent and defense of his practice. Even through all the
doubts and difficulties we can trace the vigor, the learning, the
combination of allusiveness and directness, the well-thought-out
case, the relevant use of analogy which made Callimachus what
he was. And we may admire the man who was not ashamed to be
called the jack-of-all-trades, and could claim, not without justice,
to be master of all.

V   *Summary*

We have hardly enough evidence for a real evaluation of
Callimachus as a writer of lampoons. Probably the most
memorable of such writers are those with an unrelieved
relentless single-mindedness, whether in ruthless hatred or
rumbustious obscenity. Such were Archilochus and Hipponax.
Callimachus is not of their cloth. He is reasonable and balanced.
He allows his literary opponents to make their case, allows them
to have telling points, which he proceeds to refute or counter-
weigh. He inveighs against the quarrelsomeness of scholars; in
the first poem, which sets the tone, he appears as a reconciler.
He is witty but not wounding, at the expense of the unknown
Eudemus and Philton. Even with his rivals in love, where we
might expect a more irrational intensity, we scarcely find it. The

third poem turns into a moralization about contemporary values, with a wry dig at himself. The fourth is an occasion for a fable, and though we know from the summary that Simos was charged with being a thief of handsome boys, the thrust at him is that he dares to interfere on a literary plane too high for him. In the fifth the attack on the schoolmaster is indirect and allusive: as the summarist does not know whether the teacher's name was Apollonius or Cleon, Callimachus did not even mention it. The ninth seems to have been more indirect. This is not to say that Callimachus's attacks were ineffective. The comparison of Simos to a choking briar, the ignoring of him for most of the poem, and his curt dismissal at the end are far more effective than a labored and sustained attainder which would have merely magnified his importance. When the first stirrings of the suffragette movement were making themselves felt, some male writers went to great lengths to reject their claims. Labouchère's comment "Pretty dears!", however misguided, was far more devastating.

Callimachus brought a total mastery of his medium: his versification is controlled and sure. His imagery is superb: the scholars swarming like wasps from the ground, flies on a goatherd, Delphians from a sacrifice; the spy listening in, mouth open, tongue curling like a dog when drinking; the teacher's lust a quiescent fire, but potentially runaway horses; the poet forced to eat his own homemade bread; the olive's reference to the laurel's swan song, suggesting both the truth of the last statement and the expiring of the speaker and her case; the laurel glaring like a wild bull (wit and incongruity here); the people content to scrape titbits like souvenir-hunters on Delos. It is notable how he contrives a double image, like the last, a simile within a metaphor. Equally impressive is his use of proverbial sayings. These are wittily used to the teacher:

> My friend—there's "sanctity in advice"—
> "listen to words from the heart."

Later, perhaps at the end of the same poem, he tells the man to work things out for himself: "hearers and deaf can think." The fables are in a way elaborations of the same technique.

What Callimachus does is to build into the familiar iambic meters something of the complex architecture familiar in the epinician odes of Pindar or the lyric choruses of tragedy. Three-

quarters of the poems have a myth at their core. Sometimes
those myths are aetiological, as in 7, 8, 9, and 10; sometimes they
are fables of the type found in Aesop; sometimes they are
anecdotal, like the story of Bathycles. Always they are relevant.
They are of course part of the learning he loves to show and he
keeps his learning relevant. The outstanding display of learning
was no doubt the *propempticon* for the friend who was going to
sightsee at Olympia. The poet wrote him a poem in friendship. It
was a witty poem, for it was witty to write a Baedeker in verse. It
had to be full and accurate, even to the measurements, or the wit
would fail. Full and accurate: Callimachus insisted on this. It was
Connidas not Connarus whose property is anyone's game. If you
are going to use words properly, you must respect words;
Callimachus's learning is part of his poetic creed: "We ask for the
will to learn, the gift of Hermes" (221) runs one fragment.

He knows, as always, when to write simply and directly. His
openings are vivid and direct:

Listen to Hipponax

Zeus in Elis, formed by Phidias

I'm Hermes the Passed-around, the god of Aenus

Once upon a time, with a gentle southern breeze, the *Argo*. . . .

Muses in your beauty and Apollo, to whom I pour libations.

He can be allusive when he wants to be, but his directness is
crushing—

A dog's bark—that's Eudemus.
A donkey's bray—Philton—

or touching—

Muse,
I will sing for the little girl.

Callimachus has brought together with the scazons other iambic
poems in different moods; and especially in the birthday poem

for Leon's daughter, though it is in part an exaltation of his own poetic gift, we find a warmth and tenderness which matches the familiar Heraclitus epigram.

CHAPTER 4

Lyric Poems

I   *The State of Lyric Poetry*

IT was to be expected that Callimachus with his claim to versatility would essay lyric writing, though this was not as popular in his day as it had been two centuries and more earlier. What is of particular interest is that, so far as we can see, he never tried his hand on stanzaic writing either in the forms used by Sappho and Alcaeus with such charm and power, or in the more elaborately architectural structures of Pindar. Callimachus's unit was the line, or at most the couplet; he thought in lines or couplets, and he brought to his lyrics a linear or stichic form.

It is probable that Callimachus marked off a separate book of lyrics. *The Suda* mentions one, and the summaries have four lyric poems set between *Iambi* and *Hecale*. Three of these are cited elsewhere by title. No source speaks of or cites any other lyric poem by him. Unfortunately, we have no indication at all of the length of any of the four poems. The longest fragment is from *The Deification of Arsinoe* and breaks off after 75 lines, but we do not know how much more there was to come: an account of the actual deification could have been quite lengthy. A typical scroll of Callimachus contained about 1000 lines. On the whole, it is unlikely that these lyrics extended to 250 lines each, but they may well have extended to 150 which would make in all a small but possible volume.

As with iambics, the great lyric tradition lay in the distant past. Alcman of Sparta is the first lyric poet to stand out as an individual, in the latter part of the seventh century, but in the background are shadowy figures like Olympus, a musical innovator, Terpander, and Arion. A vigorous tradition carries down into the early fifth century; then again it seems that drama took over the creative impulses, directing them into the choral songs and occasional monodies such as Creusa's song in Euripides' *Ion*. Here, however, the independent tradition never died out. Ion of Chios had lyric poetry in his varied repertoire. A musical genius named Timotheus refreshed the tradition and carried it on into the next century. Ariphron, Polyidus, Telles were writing in the early fourth century. Aristotle himself had a celebrated paean in honor of Hermeias. A Berlin papyrus (1515P) contains drinking songs which date from the fourth or early third century. In the year 300 Castorion of Soles wrote a chorus in honor of Demetrius of Phalerum, likening him to the sun. It is evident that lyric writing survived in court and ceremonial occasions: even Timotheus had found a niche in the court of Macedon. And of course we should not forget that folk song kept alive at least the awareness of lyric poetry.

II   *The Poems*

We do not even know the title of the first of the four poems, though the suggestion *To Handsome Boys* is as likely as any. We have the first line, of the poem or of the myth incorporated, a good, strong, direct beginning—

In the distant past Lemnos, beyond all other places . . .

"was happy" we can supply. The meter is the eleven-syllable line much used by Catullus later. The summary says "He addresses handsome boys. Lemnos, happy in the distant past, became unhappy when the women assaulted the men. So you (you boys) as well should not neglect the future."

The poem is evidently an example of Callimachus's use of traditional myth to point a present lesson. We know the myth from various sources. The women of Lemnos had neglected the rites of Aphrodite, who afflicted them in punishment with an intolerable stench. This turned their husbands off, who then sought consolation elsewhere. The women then murdered their husbands and the island became a community of women, ruled by Hypsipyle. When the Argonauts landed, the women took the chance of sexual union, and so restocked the population of the island. Possibly Callimachus used a version in which the men found their substitute in paederasty rather than concubinage.

This would give added relevance to the myth. But the substance of his warning is not clear. The point seems to be that happiness is followed by unhappiness. Are the boys neglecting the heterosexual love for which they are now ready? Are they provoking wives to assault their husbands? Or is it simply a general warning about mutability? Callimachus was not averse from homosexual love, and one suspects that the boys have turned him down for others, and he is trying to prove to them (and perhaps himself) that they are living in a fool's paradise.

The All-Night Festival is a drinking song in honor of Castor and Polydeuces, the Dioscuri. According to the summary, the poet also brings in their sister Helen, the type of love and beauty, asking her to accept the sacrifice. The meter was known in the ancient world as the Euripidean fourteen-syllable. The poem began with a vigorous word-picture:

> Apollo's in the chorus: I can hear the lyre:
> I recognized the Love-gods: Aphrodite too is with us.
>   (227, 1-2)

and an invitation to a drinking party:

> Come, celebrants:
> anyone who has kept awake till the very crow,

(this plainly means "climax" and must refer to some unknown game)

> he will take the prize of cakes, the prize for cottabos,
> he will kiss whatever girl whatever boy he chooses.

Cottabos was a game found in various forms which basically consisted of jerking the dregs of wine from the cup at a mark. We do not know what the prize was: it was not the same as the cakes. Other sources mention cakes and kisses as prizes: also eggs, nuts, apples, and raisins.[1]

> O Castor, O Polydeuces, horse-tamers both,
> protectors of the homeless, and escorts of the guests.
>   (227, 4-9)

More of *The Deification of Arsinoe* remains, but it is depressingly fragmentary. It is written in an anapaestic meter known as archebouleion. Arsinoe was sister and wife (in accordance with what was to become Ptolemaic practice) to Ptolemy II of Egypt. She died suddenly on July 9, 270, which gives us a close approximation to the date of the poem. The summary is curt: "He says that she was stolen away by the Dioscuri, and that an altar and precinct were set up in her honor near the Emporium"—that is, in the harbor area of Alexandria. The fragments tell us a little more. Callimachus begins by invoking Apollo and the Muses without naming them.

Let the god go first: I cannot sing without them. (228, 1)

He pictures Arsinoe swept up to heaven:

Lady, you are already under the stars of the Bear,
stolen away by the Twins, speeding past the Moon. (228, 5-6)

The scraps which follow pile on the sense of sorrow, and ancient annotators show that Callimachus continued with an aretalogy of the queen. When we pick up a continuous text it is a myth which Callimachus himself has produced. The queen's younger sister, Philotera, had died before her, and duly been deified. Callimachus pictures her as sharing a divine home with Demeter, whom he gives the ancient name of Deo, and recently returned from Enna in Sicily to Lemnos. She becomes aware of smoke drifting up from the south, and asks Charis (Grace), wife of the ugly smith-god Hephaestus who was at home on that volcanic island, to go to the summit of Mt. Athos, the snow-capped peak nearest the Pole star, and spy out the land. She first sees that the smoke is surging from Egypt, then realizes that it is not a conflagration but a funeral pyre—Arsinoe's. Charis's last speech, especially if Wilamowitz's supplements are right, begins with a stammering effect, and is punctuated by aspirations representing alike the fire and her gasping horror:

"Do not cry for your country: your Pharos is not aflame
with fire." (228, 67-8)

The manuscript breaks off, and we do not know whether the poet simply described the dedication of the holy precinct or went into the whole deification. The poem is of considerable historical interest, and a brief consideration of the banal productions of successive Poets Laureate in Britain on similar occasions is enough to put Callimachus on a merited eminence.

Branchus has an equally curt summary: "Apollo comes from Delos to a place near Miletus called the Sacred Grove, where Branchus was." We know something of the legendary Branchus, descended from Apollo himself on his mother's side, and one of Apollo's priests on his father's. He was a favorite of Apollo who gave him the gift of prophecy. At Didyma near Miletus he founded an oracular shrine of Apollo which attained an international reputation. Callimachus writes of this in choriam- bics, long lines with a basic unit ♩ ♪♪♩, a rhythm later used with great skill by Horace. He begins as usual with an invocation which plunges straight in:

> Powers worthy of hymns, Phoebus and Zeus, founders of Didyma.
> (229, 1).

We pick up with Phoebus addressing Branchus, and calling him from a shepherd's life to one of prophecy.

> "That damnable devastating plague shall not assail the
>   flocks of animals,
> young man (my heart loves you dearly)." (229, 2-3)

He commends his ancestry.

> So you said, Phoebus; his heart leaped up at your gifts.
> He gave you a glorious shrine in the wood of your epiphany,
> close to the twin springs, planting the laurel bough.
> (229, 9-10)

Callimachus invokes the god himself with a typical explanatory comment.

> Be kindly, Lord Delphinius, I begin with that title,
> since a dolphin carried you from Delos to the city of Oecus.
> (229, 11-21)

Oecus must be Miletus. The theme of the poem, the exposition of the myth behind a temple-founding, suited Callimachus perfectly. The song may have been commissioned from Miletus, but it cannot have been an unwelcome commission.

III *Summary*

We should not be much the poorer if no trace of these lyrics had survived. They were in no sense a major part of Callimachus's output. The poem on Arsinoe is of interest for nonpoetic reasons. But all four lyrics are a further testimony to Callimachus's versatility. If they do not sweep us from our feet, as Sappho may, or Pindar; neither do they disappoint us. It is not possible to point the finger and say "Here is a weakness." For Callimachus is a craftsman; that is his great strength; and he touched nothing that he did not master.

CHAPTER 5

Hecale

I *Epic and Epyllion*

THE great age of epic lay far in the past. *The Iliad* and *The Odyssey* alone survive intact. They represent the culmination of a bardic tradition of formulaic composition, as we now know, improvised orally on preexisting materials. The new insights thrown on bardic methods by comparative studies in the Balkans across the past fifty years make clear that we would not expect to find survivals from the pre-Homeric period. The Homeric poems are now dated to the eighth century B.C., and their survival has something to do with the introduction of an alphabetical script, combined with the emergence of fresh cultural patterns which meant that the bardic poems must be recorded or perish.

A number of other epics roughly contemporary with *The Iliad* and *The Odyssey*, somewhat shorter, though still substantial, long survived though they have now perished. Three dealt with the traditions of Thebes, *The Oedipodea, The Thebaid,* and *The Epigoni,* four with the Trojan cycle, the oddly named *Cypria, The Aethiopis, The Sack of Troy,* and *The Little Iliad;* we should perhaps add Eugammon's *Telegonica,* a continuation of *The Odyssey* in which invention came in alongside tradition; this, however, dates from the sixth century, and represents the end of that phase. *The Capture of Oechalia* provided Sophocles with a theme, and Callimachus with a chance to show his prowess as a literary historian in identifying Creophylus as its author.[1] Other works are more shadowy—*The Battle with the Titans,* the stories of Alcmaeon, Heracles, Danaus, the Argonauts, and others. Epic composition continued down into the fifth century. It was in part governed by local patriotism. Each of the major cities had to have its epic. The anonymous *Phoronis* provided this for Argos, a noble poet named Eumelus helped Corinth to find its identity, Panyassis of Halicarnassus wrote in the traditions of Ionia,

Diphilus gave Athens an epic about Theseus. Of these we know that Diphilus belonged to the fifth century, and Panyassis, uncle to the historian Herodotus, met a violent death in 460. Choerilus of Samos is the most interesting of this group. Right at the beginning of his poem he envies the poets who lived in the days when the fields were still untrodden. Now everything is in decline, the scope of art has narrowed. Choerilus, while embarking on the use of Homeric techniques for an account of Persian history, recognizes that that mode of composition is past.

One other figure must be mentioned, if only because he was one of Callimachus's *bêtes noires*. This was Antimachus of Colophon. We cannot date him precisely, but he was writing in the fifth century and was dead by the middle of the fourth, and maybe well before that. He wrote an epic poem on Thebes and an immense elegiac poem on an epic scale, *Lyde,* in which he paid tribute to the girl he loved in an elaborate working out of legendary stories of unhappy love, strung together in an artistic whole. In this we can see Antimachus as a precursor of the Hellenistic Age, and Callimachus's intensity suggests that he recognized in Antimachus something of himself: after all, Antimachus was not doing anything very different from that which Callimachus achieved in his *Aitia.*

Two contemporaries of Callimachus essayed epic writing of the old school. The epic by Apollonius "the Rhodian" was mythological, taking up the story of the Argonauts. It is long enough, but nothing like as long as the Homeric epics. Unfortunately, we cannot now disentangle what is original in Apollonius and what he borrowed from the lost work of predecessors, though at one point the scholiast gives us explicit information that Apollonius took from a predecessor his account of the adventures of the hero Sthenelus, but himself invented the appearance of Sthenelus's ghost and the subsequent offering of sacrifice to appease the angry spirit. It is likely that a similar combination of scholarly derivation and original coloring suffused the rest of the work. Apollonius's poem is in many ways the product of its age—the care with which he investigates previous treatments; the element of the adventure story, which was soon to take shape in the first novels; the selectivity which singled out less-known episodes in the myth; the love affair; and particularly the psychological interest in the awakening of love in Medea, which is the most successful thing in the poem. It is

easy to criticize Apollonius. His poem lacks the narrative drive
needed to sustain epic and the unity of structure needed for a
briefer story. Certainly we can see that Callimachus would
wheel away from it. But Apollonius has positive qualities; his
poem is readable, and still read. His is a *tour-de-force*.
Callimachus was right: there was no future here, at least not for
the Greeks. Apollonius gave epic a brief present.

Rhianus came from Crete, but certainly spent some time in
Alexandria. We know little about him, but he must belong to the
period of Callimachus. He wrote a historical epic on the
Messenian Wars (as did another of whom we know even less,
Aeschylus of Alexandria). It was a good subject, historical yet
heroic, adventurous, dramatic and set in dramatic scenery. He
must have visited Messenia, and the tradition that he was born in
Ithome was no doubt a false deduction from this. He fancied
himself as a modern Homer. Aristomenes is his Achilles,
struggling against hostile destiny, patriotic and noble. Little of
the original poem has survived, but we can discern something of
it through the fourth book of Pausanias, wbo used Rhianus as a
source for the Messenian Wars. Rhianus was original in his choice
of subject, occasionally philosophical and moralizing in his
treatment, the child of his time in the introduction of learning,
psychology, digression, but ultimately derivative and imitative.
Still, centuries later the Roman Manilius could mention him in
the same breath as Homer (3, 1).

Callimachus was revolutionary in opposing the long poem and
claiming that even narrative poems should be short and polished.
Theocritus followed him in this:

> I have a deep hatred for the builder who seeks
> to erect a house level with Mt. Orymedon's peak,
> and for those chickens of the Muses who waste
> their efforts crowing to rival the poet of Chios. (7, 45-8)

The words are inappropriate to Lycidas, and are a gratuitous
expression of Theocritus's own view. In the thirteenth and
twenty-second *Idylls* Theocritus took episodes from *The
Argonautica* and reworked them in the spirit of the epyllion; in
the twenty-fourth he wrote a prize poem on Heracles in the
same mood. Exactly where *Hecale* fits into the sequence we do

not know, but Callimachus was the driving force behind the
change in narrative poetry.

II   Hecale

Hecale was Callimachus's answer to his critics. They claimed
that he was no real poet because incapable of composing on a
large scale.[2] It was an answer, yet in a curious way it was a refusal
to answer; it was a demonstration of what he believed ought to
replace the long poem. We do not know how long *Hecale* was.
The most substantial fragment consists of about 70 lines with
lacunae of a further 56. It contains an incidental episode which is
not even mentioned in the summary, and which can hardly have
been more than a small fraction of the whole, perhaps an eighth.
On the other hand, *Hecale* occupied no more than a single scroll.
We can reasonably assume a poem of about 1000 lines, enough to
prove his competence in the medium without compromising his
principles.

The primary myth he selected was the story of the Athenian
hero Theseus taming the Bull of Marathon. Callimachus took the
story from Philochorus or one of the other chroniclers of the
traditions of Attica, but the summary shows that he treated it
with some poetic freedom. The hero escaped from Medea,
proved himself his father's son by arriving in Athens with the
sword and boots Aegeus had left for him, but was now the apple
of his father's eye and allowed no freedom. Wanting to challenge
the bull, he slipped out secretly. Caught in a storm, he sheltered
in a hut occupied by an old woman named Hecale, who
welcomed him warmly. Next morning he rose early, over-
powered the bull, and returned to Hecale. He had promised to
repay her hospitality. He found her dead and established a deme
named after her, and a shrine to Zeus Hecaleios.

In centering his story on the old peasant woman, the poet is
joining in the assertion of simplicity against city-life. But in
addition to this framework Callimachus showed his skill in
weaving several stories together, and he incorporated the myth
of Erichthonius, the divine child whom Athene wanted to bring
up in secret; she placed the child in a chest and entrusted this to
the daughters of Cecrops, king of Athens, with injunctions not to
open the chest. She went off to fetch a hill to give the Acropolis

added strength. They disobeyed, and saw the child with two snakes. A crow met her with the news, she dropped the hill, which stands apart from the Acropolis and is now Lycabettus, and punished the crow as the bringer of bad news, with banishment from the Acropolis.

Unfortunately, most of the surviving fragments are single phrases, which give us no idea of the continuity or the poet's narrative skill, and it is impossible to know where many of them fitted in at all. He began directly; Callimachus's openings are as direct as those for which Aristophanes pilloried Euripides.

Once on a time a woman of Attica lived on a hill of Erechtheus. (230)

Even there Callimachus is careful with his scholarship; he uses the archaic Actaee for Attica.

> All travelers
> loved her for her hospitality; she kept open house. (231)

Her name indeed became proverbial for hospitality, and occasioned more than one false etymology for Hecale.

The next episode (we do not know how Callimachus managed the transition) showed Medea's attempt on Theseus's life; she had recognized him as Aegeus's son. She tried to poison him: the curt cry which saved him "Stop, boy, don't drink" (233) survives.

From there to Athens, where Aegeus welcomed his son's unexpected arrival, and there was some kind of flashback to the episode where he had placed his sword ("a blade from Aedepsus" where there were iron and copper mines, an ancient Toledo) and boots under a rock, for the boy Theseus when he became strong enough to lift the covering: other versions tell us that the sword and boots authenticated Theseus as the king's son.

Theseus stole away from home on his adventure. It was a glorious day, but towards evening a storm began to pile up. Through the remnants of the passages we can discern the poet's capacity for evocative writing:

> While it was still high noon and the earth warm,
> the dazzling sky remained clearer than crystal,

> there was no wisp of mist in sight, the sky lay
> cloudless . . .
> When the mother . . . the girls
> begin to ask for their supper and lay aside their work,
> then . . .
> first over Parnes, then nearer massing on the ridge
> of thyme-scented Aegaleos, it stood bringing much rain.
> A double . . .
> of rocky Hymettus . . .
> lightning was flashing . . .
> as when the tempest breaks . . .
> over the Ausonian sea . . .
> and the scudding gale from Merithus to the north
> assailed the clouds . . . (238, 15–30)

The geography is precise. The storm is coming from the northwest. Theseus first becomes aware of the blotting out of Parnes, the high mountain to the north. Then as it encroaches on the plain it masses on the low ridge to the west of Athens. Finally, it engulfs city and plain and reaches the bare rocky mass of Hymettus, famed for its honey, which lies to the east of the city. Two unplaced fragments probably belong here and enhance the description—the reptiles hiding in their holes (336) and the lamps guttering (269).

When we next encounter Theseus he is shaking out his wet clothes in Hecale's hut. It is simply furnished. One of the features of Alexandrian writing was the realism, the simple, homely, down-to-earth, amusing, practical, unheroic realism with which they invested their pictures of the heroic age. Callimachus was no exception, but characteristically he also establishes links with the account of Odysseus in the swineherd's hut in *The Odyssey*. His description of the simple food is meticulous; he distinguishes between the large olives plucked when unripe and left to mature, and the pale olives which were salted down (248). Among other pleasing touches is:

> She took from the bin and set before him plenty of rolls—
> the sort that women keep in reserve for herdsmen. (251)

After supper they talked and Callimachus used the opportunity for flashbacks and diversification. We have lost Theseus's narrative, but the conclusion is noble in its courtesy.

"I'm going down to Marathon to ...
... Pallas is my escort.
So I've answered your questions. Now let me,
mother, I want to hear a little bit from you.
... you're an old woman living in a lonely spot." (253, 1-5)

Most of Hecale's reply is lacking, but there is an excellent description of some unknown person out of her past:

Horses brought him from Aphidnae ...
that's what he was like, and Zeus's sons ...
I remember the beauty of ...
a cloak fastened with clasps of gold,
spiders' work ... (253, 8-12)

She is proud of her past, proudly asserts that there was no poverty in her family, no inherited penury. She had her own threshing floor with hired hands to look after it. Eventually they turn in to sleep; she has her own bed in the corner (256), Theseus lies down by the fire (like Odysseus) with a stone for pillow (375).

He arose early. She heard him stirring, and herself got up to see him off. Probably we should fit in here a fine visual picture, perhaps his last view of her:

The broad-brimmed hat projecting from the forehead suited her,
felted, shepherds' wear: she had a stick in her hand. (292)

This whole account of Theseus in Hecale's hut made a great impression on Callimachus's readers, and several poets offered it the tribute of imitation.[3]

The actual encounter with the bull was treated with dispatch: it was a piece of Callimachus's wit to make his centerpiece the fellowship of Theseus and Hecale, not the heroic exploit, and by contrast with that leisurely episode to show his capacity for swift narrative. The only quotation shows the hero forcing down the bull's horn (258); next we find him dragging it behind him, "an unenthusiastic traveler," as it is delightfully described. A fragment of greater length describes the reaction of the people of Marathon.

> He fastened the other belt and attached his sword.
> When they saw this, they were all scared to death
> to be face to face with the mighty hero and the monstrous beast,
> till Theseus shouted to them from a distance:
> "Don't be afraid. Don't run away. Send your fastest runner
> to take a message to my father Aegeus in the city.
> Tell him—it will ease his mind greatly:
> 'Theseus is not far off. He is bringing the bull alive
> from the lush fields of Marathon.' " They heard his words
> and all raised the shout of victory, and stood their ground.
> The south wind does not scatter leaves so copiously,
> even the north wind when the fall is fully come can't compare
> with the leaves those country folk scattered over Theseus,
> thronging round him in a circle, while the women
> . . . garlanded him with girdles . . . (260, 1–15)

Pelting a victor with leaves was a common celebration; Callimachus combines it with a visual parallel drawn from nature.

At this point about twenty lines are missing, and when we return to legibility, an old crow is telling a young one the story of Erichthonius; it is particularly frustrating not to know how Callimachus handled the transition.

>   "But Pallas
> left Hephaestus's child for a long period within a chest
> (till she could fetch the rock for the children of Cecrops),
> an ineffable mystery. I was not told his parentage.
> I did not know till a rumor spread among the primeval
> birds that Earth in fact bore him to Hephaestus.
> At that time she wanted to establish a strong point for the land
> which she had lately won by the votes of Zeus
> and the rest of the Twelve Immortals, and the snake's evidence.
> So she was making for Pellene in Achaea. Meanwhile, the girls
> in charge of the chest planned to commit a sinful act
> . . . they unfastened the lock on the chest." (260, 18–28)

The reference to Athene's victory over Poseidon for the land of Attica is typically allusive. Here we should fit in a passage which tells of the crow's meeting with Athene, as, dressed for business, she is carrying the rock (261), and two descriptions of her fury, "crammed brimful with anger" (320) and "turning white and glaring with eyes askance" (374). She banishes the crows: "Athene's anger is oppressive and unending," he comments ruefully. Callimachus makes a neat point:

> "I was there, quite small at the time. I'm now
> in my eighth generation, my parents' tenth." (260, 42–4)

In folklore the crow lived to ten generations; Aegeus was eighth in line from Cecrops. Callimachus built into his bird-narrative other items of bird-lore, the stork as bird of vengeance, the crow eating barley with brief *aition* of the barley-groats slopping over from the posset, the raven once white being turned black by Apollo because he brought the god the news of his lover Coronis's infidelity, the granting to crows of the gift of prophecy. Again the weaving together of myths is one of the poet's skills. The section ends with an excellent account of the world awakening to work.

> They dropped off to sleep—only briefly, for soon there appeared
> the frosty half-light of dawn, when the hands of thieves are no
>   longer
> after victims; the torches of day are beginning to glow.
> Men drawing water are singing the Song of the Windlass.
> The man with his house by the roadside is waked by the creaking
> of the axles of carts, and many have their hearing
> harried by the blacksmith's apprentices, oblivious to sound.
>   (260, 63–69)

It is a nice touch: normally the birds waken the men; here the men waken the birds.

Theseus returned to Hecale's cottage to find the neighbors preparing her grave. Here is a fragment of a funeral oration, given by Theseus or some other, warm and appreciative:

> Go, kindly woman,
> along the road cares and griefs do not tread.
>   ... often,
> mother ... we will recall the hospitality
> of your cottage. It was a shelter open to all. (263)

Theseus commemorated her by three acts, two of which are given in the summary. He established a banquet in her honor, named a deme or political and geographical subunit after her, and built a sanctuary to Zeus Hecaleios or Hecalus. A feature of the celebration was that she was addressed by the pet name Hecaline; she had seemingly used similar language to Theseus.[4] The central episode in Callimachus's poem is thus an *aition* of these later cult practices.

This is the outline of the narrative as we can reconstruct it. But there are over a hundred quotations whose place is uncertain, some of which undoubtedly belong to the conversation between Theseus and Hecale. Such are the references to the bandit Cercyon whom Theseus killed (284A, 10) in a place

> where wrestling-grounds
> cruel to strangers flow with crimson blood. (328)

There are a number of references to the areas around Argos. Probably this is the town of which it is said:

> So dead men carry no coin as fare
> in this city only. Elsewhere it's the rule to carry
> a coin in their desiccated mouths. (278)

There must have beeen an *aition* for this, that the people of Aegialus were let off the fare across the river of death because they told Demeter about the rape of Persephone. There are other references to these divinities, "Deo and hospitable Clymenus's wife" (285). Clymenus is Lord of the Dead, ironically described as hospitable, his wife is Persephone, or as she is called in one fragment (302) Deoine. A line and a half speak of yet another myth, the story of how Nisus, King of Megara, depended for his security on a purple lock of hair, and how his daughter Scylla, in love with his enemy Minos of Crete, cut if off, and how they were turned into birds.[5]

> Scylla, a whore who lived up to her name,
> reaped the purple lock of hair. (288)

The word "reaped" is pointed: she reaped a harvest of trouble. This was perhaps part of Theseus's account of his journey from

Troezen to Athens. To that same narrative presumably belongs
the reference to the lion of Nemea (339). But we do not know
where to fit in an account of a child winning ten knucklebones as
a prize (276).

Other passages add something to our appreciation of
Callimachus's power with words. One line, which breaks off
tantalizingly, describes two children running up and down (284A,
7). They are compared with shuttles on a loom, an excellent
image, but the shuttles seem to be operating in a ravine. If this is
right, it is bold metaphor for the gap through which the shuttles
pass. The word for *shuttles* can also mean *aspens*, which fit the
ravine literally, but the children's movement less well. A number
of passages show careful observation:

> when cows, native to the land,
> chew poppy-blossom and golden wheat (277)

and

> round his head he wore a circular
> felt hat, new from Thessaly, to protect him
> from the heat of high noon (304)

and (though this is of doubtful authenticity)

> he sought on foot
> to mount the ridge above the glens. All the rocks
> were sheer below, and there was no way up (309)

and

> an old woman's lips are always on the go (310)

and

> flour
> carelessly prepared by the miller's daughter with husks left in.
> (334)

We have a touch of country talk: the goad is called "the cow's
gadfly" (301) and snatches of gnomic wisdom:

> Eyes may be ignorant but ears know (282)

and

> God did not grant
> laughter without tears to human weakness (298)

and

> If justice has not
> caught up with you in punishment, she'll be twice as stern
> when she comes again among the dead. (358)

Such passages, just because of their isolation, allow us to see with a sharper eye Callimachus's peculiar qualities.

III   *Summary*

Hecale rates with *Aitia* as Callimachus's supreme achievement. It was immensely influential; it was, as Trypanis says, "read, copied, paraphrased and commented on up to the thirteenth century A.D." Further, it set the tone for the Hellenistic epyllion. We may instance the poem, wrongly attributed to Theocritus (25), telling the story of Heracles and the Nemean lion. The episode itself may have been suggested by the story of Theseus and the Bull of Marathon (possibly also by Callimachus's treatment of the lion of Nemea in *Aitia*), and it has a similar genre setting. Our scanty awareness of the Hellenistic epyllion is sufficient for us to realize how much we have lost. There is *Actaeon,* referred to by Apollodorus (3, 4, 4). There are tantalizing papyrus fragments dealing with the labors of Heracles, the rescue of Andromeda, Telephus, Diomedes, and others.[6] Enough survives of the last-named to enable us to see it as a typical Alexandrian epyllion, with realism and mythology rubbing shoulders, and learned descriptions of the beauty of hounds, and delightful pictures of dogs wagging their tails to greet a visitor, and of an old man dropping to the ground with distress, then recovering himself, standing upright and escorting the visitor in. A fragment by a known and influential poet, Euphorion,[7] seems to be part of an epyllion on Heracles, derivative from *Hecale* and other parts of Callimachus. Moschus and Parthenius are later exponents of Callimachean techniques. So, among the Romans was Catullus, and later Ovid, who in fact adapted *Hecale* for his episode of Philemon and Baucis in *Metamorphoses* (8, 611–724).

Three references from Roman times will serve to show the continuing impact of the poem. One comes from an anonymous song to Priapus (12):

> Younger she than Hector's mother,
> sister of the Sibyl of Cumae,
> like in age to her whom Theseus
> found, returning, on the pyre.

The second comes from Petronius's *Satyricon* (135):

Such a hostess there was once in the land of Attica,
worthy of the rites offered Hecale, whom the Muse of Cyrene's poet
in his eloquent age passed down for future generations to honor.

The third and most striking is an epigram in *The Greek Anthology*, accompanying a copy of *Hecale* which Crinagoras, a poet from Mytilene, is presenting to Augustus's nephew M. Claudius Marcellus, the same whose premature death Vergil alluded to so touchingly as to reduce his imperial listeners to tears:

> This chiselled poem's by Callimachus: in it he let out
>   every reef of his Muse.
> He sings of Hecale's hospitable hut, and the labors imposed
>   on Theseus at Marathon.
> May the young strength of his hands be yours, Marcellus,
>   and a like glory in life. (9, 545)

CHAPTER 6

Miscellaneous Poems

I Introduction

WE have fragments of, or references to, a number of miscellaneous poems. Unfortunately, summaries of these poems have not survived. We have therefore no idea how they fitted into the scheme of Callimachus's collected works. We do, however, know that the hymns and epigrams (the latter perhaps even added posthumously) came at the very end of the collection, so that it seems best to group what is known of the others in a single section here. The absence of the summaries gravely limits our knowledge of their place in the series of publications.

II Galatea

We know of one, and only one, other epic poem by Callimachus besides *Hecale;* this was entitled *Galatea.*[1] Even here we are standing on uncertain ground. We know that there was a poem called *Galatea,* and that it was in hexameters from a typical piece of ichthyological learning:

> or (better) the sacred fish with the gilt head
> or the perch and all those others produced by the sea's
> illimitable depths. (378)

It is a reasonable deduction that the poem was a mythological epyllion about the sea nymph Galatea. Polyphemus's monstrous infatuation for her has its place elsewhere in Alexandrian poetry, and indeed in one of Callimachus's own epigrams.[2] We have no hint of any kind to tell us how the poet handled his theme.

But there is a further indication about the poem. An unplaced fragment in hexameters speaks of

> those whom Brennus led from the ocean in the west
> aiming to crush the Greeks. (379)

This certainly seems heroic poetry, extracted from some epic, and we know of no other epic from which it could have been derived. Brennus was commander-in-chief of the Gauls who invaded Greece in 279–278. The Gauls, or Galatai, had their mythological descent from Galatea through her son, the eponymous Galates. In this way we can see a relevant thread of connection, wholly in keeping with the poet's practice, between a historical event and a mythological origin. Brennus was wounded at Delphi, later committing suicide. This is sufficient reason for attributing to this poem one other hexameter fragment:

> Pallas, when Delphi was erecting her statue as Pronaia. (592)

Athene was called Pro-naia, because she had her statue Before-the-temple (of Apollo), but the name was blurred and blended with Pronoia or Providence, and we can glimpse here all manner of possibilities for Callimachus, even if we do not know how he took them up.

Unfortunately, we cannot certainly relate *Galatea* to *Hecale*. We can say *Galatea* must be after 278, but that leaves thirty years or so in which it might have been produced. *Hecale* cannot have ben early, since it was written in answer to criticism of *Aitia*. Probably it is best to assume that *Galatea* was written shortly after the Gauls' invasion, and sparked off by those events, in which case it is probably the earlier of the two. In that case it was not regarded by the poet's critics as a sufficient demonstration of his mastery of the medium. But there remains the possibility that after *Hecale* he essayed a short epyllion using a different approach and technique.

III   *New Uses for Elegy*

In the remains of elegiac verse we can see Callimachus as a daring innovator in the use of the meter of which he was acknowledged master. We no longer have the rigid conceptions of poetic genre which dominated the ancient world, but we shall not appreciate Callimachus's achievement unless we recognize his originality in breaking through conventional patterns. There is a parallel in Callimachus's Roman disciple Catullus. To us he is one of the world's great lyric poets; yet Quintilian does not count him worth a mention among the lyric poets of Rome, because with the exception of one wedding song and two Sapphics (one a translation) Catullus did not write in the conventional lyric meters, but poured out the emotions fitted to lyric poetry into the meters generally used for lampoons and frivolous or occasional verse, rather as if someone tried to write love poetry in limericks. Callimachus wanted to revive a form of poetry which was obsolescent, the epinician ode, or poem in honor of a victor at the great athletic festivals. These were associated with lyric meters. There was no longer a choir readily available to sing such an ode, and Callimachus was never a mere antiquarian. He tried to revive the epinician poem in the elegiac meter: it was after all a singularly flexible medium in its moods.

The most interesting survival here is a long extract, with unfortunate gaps, covering in all a little under a hundred lines, of an epinician elegy in honor of Sosibius. Sosibius was an Egyptian, born in the reign of Ptolemy I, who came into political prominence in the reign of Ptolemy III, was one of the leading statesmen under Ptolemy IV, and died as an old but still active figure shortly before 200. Evidently Sosibius had been something of an athlete in his younger days; he had won the two-lap race for boys at the Ptolemaea, a festival established in the name of Ptolemy I in 279–278, and while still under age had won the men's wrestling at the Panathenaic festival. Later, after he had given up active personal participation, he continued to take a vicarious interest, and, when he had acquired the position and resources, was able to enter a team of African horses (Callimachus calls them Asbystian, from a tribe in Cyrenaica, but this is not to be taken literally) and win the prestigious chariot-race at both the Nemea and the Isthmia, the first Egyptian to score such a double first. In writing of him, Callimachus must have had in mind some of the great rulers of the Sicilian cities, whose victories in similar events called out all Pindar's eloquence, and perhaps still more the achievement of Alcibiades in attaining first, second, and fourth place at Olympia, which drew a song from Euripides, with whom Callimachus had other affinities. He was not afraid to stand comparison with any man.

Yet Callimachus's offering is decidedly odd. The old epinician odes were noted for their incorporation of myths into their song of triumph. Callimachus was fascinated by mythology and a supremely skilled exponent of its use in poetry. Yet there is no trace of a myth in the surviving fragment. This may be accidental, but it is certainly strange. Secondly, Sosibius was minister to a powerful dynasty, and Callimachus was something of a courtier. Yet there is no mention, in what we have, of any of the Ptolemies.

For what remains we can admire the skill without being attracted. The poem is too carefully programmed, like Horace's *Carmen Saeculare*. The skill consists in fitting the program into smoothly flowing verses; it moves our admiration but not our emotion. The first of the two victories was at the Isthmia, and Callimachus recalls the song of praise on that occasion, which called on Poseidon, the patron of Corinth with its two harbors:

> "O god, enthroned on both sides of the sea-girt narrows,
>   by whom the sons of Sisyphus took their oaths of old,
> Lord of the holy isthmus where the land of Pelops tapers,
>   with Cromna on one side, Lechaeon on the other,
> where they judge hand and foot and swift horse
>   in full equity, and true judgment outruns gold,
> gold, the beautiful, evil gift of the ants to men."
>
>   (384, 9–15)

It is a warning to a rich man.

> He sped to Nemea, and promptly brought celery crowns
>   from Argos to add to those from Pirene,
> so that anyone living in the land of Alexander or by Cinyps
>   may learn that Sosibius won two crowns,
> alongside the two children, Learchus's brother,
>   and Myrina's daughter's fosterchild,
> so that the Nile as it brings its annual fertilizing flood
>   may say "A glorious gift from my own child!
>   . . . never yet has any brought to my city a double
>   prize from these funeral games
>   . . . rich as I am—and no mortal man knows

> where I journey from—in this alone I was poorer
> than those brooks which women's white ankles have no problem
> in crossing, or children on foot with knees dry."
>
> (384, 21-34)

The allusions are contorted. The crowns from Argos refer to the Nemean Games. Pirene was a famous fountain in Corinth, near where the Isthmian Games were held. Alexander's city is of course Alexandria, an easy riddle; the Cinyps is the river which separated Cyrenaica from Carthaginian territory, an allusion to the marriage of Ptolemy III to Berenice of Cyrene in 247 which united Cyrenaica to Egypt. Learchus's brother is Melicertes, the hero honored at the Isthmia; at the Nemea they honored Opheltes, fosterling of Myrina's daughter Hypsipyle; both festivals were said to originate in funerary games. The annual Nile flood was the life of Egypt, which was sometimes called "the gift of the Nile"; the sources of the river remained unexplored in the ancient world. The Nile is jealous of miserable little streams (in comparison) whose citizens have triumphed in the games, and proud of Sosibius as a true-born Egyptian. The whole is an excellent specimen of Alexandrianism. We are not to suppose that contemporary readers would have grasped every reference.

The poet adverted to Sosibius's earlier victories, and showed a particular interest in the monuments celebrating the new triumphs. At Argos there was a statue of the Graces ("daughters of Eurynome") robed, not as usual nude. Near Pelusium was a bronze chariot, whose raw metal came from Cyprus. The surviving passage ends with flattery which contains implicit political advice:

> we sing him for his victories; he knows what will bring peace
>   to the people, and does not forget the humble,
> a trait rarely discerned in a man of wealth,
>   whose mind cannot rise above his fortune.
> My praise cannot match his merits, but I'll not forget him:
>   either way I'd fear the people's censure. (384, 54-9)

The other epinician elegy is also for a chariot-race at Nemea, but we do not know the date or victor. The scanty fragments are not without interest. The beginning owes something to Pindar, but shows Callimachus's liking for plunging straight into his subject.

I owe a thank-offering to Zeus and Nemea. (383, 1)

There is an allusive reference to bees as "cattle-born creatures," an ancient error familiar from the last book of Vergil's *Georgics*, where Aristaeus restocks his hive from such a carcass. The horses are described in a not-yet-faded simile as running like the winds, so that none can discern the trace of their passage. The poem contained a reference to the mourning rites in Egypt for the bull Apis.

Another experimental use for the elegiac couplet was an epithalamium for Queen Arsinoe. At least this is a reasonable speculation. We have the opening line:

Stranger, I am embarking on a song for Arsinoe's marriage. (392)

It happens that we know of only one other epithalamium in elegiacs, and that was written for this same marriage by Posidippus, so, although we cannot be totally sure that Callimachus's poem was not in hexameters, it is likely that this too was an experimental use of his specialized medium.

IV   *Other Elegiac Poems*

The other fragmentary remains of known poems need not, indeed cannot detain us long. The most interesting and frustrating is mentioned and quoted in an anonymous treatise on metrics. The poem was called *The Archive* and the two lines which survive are a powerful account of the mordant poet Archilochus:

He drew on the hound's fierce anger and the wasp's sharp sting, with the venom of both on his lips. (380)

That is good writing, and good, though not original, criticism. We must deduce the contents of the whole work from this and from the title. It may have been a sustained work of literary criticism or (perhaps more likely) a survey of poets of the past, with epigrammatic comments on each. C. Dilthey in *Analecta Callimachea* drew a possible comparison with Varro's *Imagines*.

The only other quotation from one of the elegiac poems was written in honor of Berenice, but we do not know the occasion or the full subject of the poem. The lines are vigorous and contain a typical reference to a historical legend that the Phocaeans, besieged by the Persians in 540 BC, sailed for the west, throwing a lump of red-hot iron into the sea, and swearing never to return until it reemerged:[3]

> till the mighty red-hot ore of the Phocaeans appears in the sea,
>   till Pallas gives birth, and Artemis marries,
> . . . for ever the very best is in store . . . for Berenice.
>   (388, 9-11)

More important than either of these was *Ibis*, and it is curious that this has been totally lost. *The Suda* tells us that it was a poem of deliberate obscurity and hostility to an enemy whom he called Ibis or the Ibis: this was Apollonius, author of *The Argonautica*. Strabo gives an account of the ibis in his section on the flora and fauna of Egypt. "Tamest of all is the ibis. In shape and size it resembles a stork. It is found in two colors, one like the stork, the other pure black. They congregate at every crossroads in Alexandria. They are at the same time useful and detrimental, useful because they pick up all kinds of vermin and the leftovers from the butchers' shops and fishmongers', detrimental because they are omnivorous and unclean and it is not easy to keep them away from all that is clean and is not to be polluted" (17, 283). We can see here the grounds for Callimachus's rejection of Apollonius, and his identification of him with the ibis. He regarded his younger contemporary as one who followed the beaten track, the main road, and as one who took promising themes and fouled them up. In one of his most famous epigrams he himself claimed to avoid the main road and the common spring; in the *Hymn to Apollo* he contrasted the pure and unsullied water of true inspiration with the flotsam and jetsam of the great rivers of Mesopotamia.[4]

Ovid took this idea and title of his hate-poem *Ibis* straight from Callimachus, as he explicitly declares

> As Battus's son cursed his enemy as Ibis
> so I curse you and yours. (55-6)

Unfortunately, the one thing that we can be certain of in the relation between the two poems is that the idea and title were all that Ovid derived from his precursor, and that his poem therefore cannot help us to reconstruct the earlier work. It remains a lacuna in our knowledge, to be filled only speculatively. But we may wryly reflect that when the editors of that once popular anthology *The Week-End Book* divided their selection of poetry between Great Poems, State Poems, Hate Poems, Love Poems, and Epigrams, they were almost offering us an analytical table of Callimachus's verse.

V   *Miscellaneous Fragments*

There are several hundreds of fragments of verse by Callimachus whose original source is not known. Most of them are from hexameter verse or elegiacs; a few are in iambics or other forms. They are cited because they contain rare words, or grammatical peculiarities, or place references, or pieces of lore, or quotably epigrammatic pronouncements, or for similar reasons. They are not necessarily representative of his writing, therefore, though in fact their general effect is to reinforce what we know from other parts of his work.

Some touch on his poetic creed. He is prodigal with his poetry, "no miser with the Muses" (538). He would not withhold from knowledge anything good (620). He proudly affirms the learning which informs his pen: "my poems are well researched" (612). He is suspicious of the parentage of poetry which is too comfortably popular: "the songs which prospered were bastard" (604). Naturally, in view of the circumstances of survival, we have plenty of opportunities of discerning his curious learning, and especially his interest in religious and mythological origins. We have the sacrifice of donkeys to Phoebus in the far north (492), sacrifice without fire to the Muses (494), the offering of "sober honeycakes" to the Furies (681), the women spitting in their laps at the name of Nemesis (687); we have the Thessalian practice of dragging murderers around their victims' graves (588); we have two references to the Pythagoreans, one about their refusal to divulge their mystic secrets (533), the other about their abstention from beans (553). This is all linked to Callimachus's practice of allusive reference. The sky is called "the circling son of Acmon" (498): Acmon, father of Ouranos, was according to different versions a name for the aether (or upper air), or for Oceanus, the river surrounding the land-mass of the earth. Sometimes the reference defeats us.

> She saw her sister Inatia during the act of childbirth. (524)

Inatia is Ilithyia, goddess of childbirth; the sister then must be Hebe, goddess of youth. But who is giving birth? Ilithyia, who in one tradition was mother of Eros? Hebe, who was married to Heracles? Or some third mother, perhaps Leto, mother of Apollo and Artemis? Simpler, and more delightful, is the description of the priestesses of the Furies as "sober" because their offerings were without wine (681) or the use of the phrase "the heel-driven horse" to describe the potter's wheel (670).

There is a certain amount of local color in the fragments. Some of it refers to his native land of Cyrene, which he calls his mother:

> Ladies of Libya, demi-goddesses, who guard
> the halls and long shores of the Nasamones,
> grant my mother power and vitality. (602)

In another passage it is fatherland, and he refers with antiquarian lore to its founding from Santorini:

> Formerly Calliste, later named Thera,
> mother of our fatherland with its horses. (716)

Then there are references to Egypt, to a tree called *mimusops* which the hero Perseus is said to have naturalized in Egypt (655), or to an entrance-way sacred to the jackal-god Anubis (715).

Callimachus liked to introduce traditional gnomic wisdom, like "the purse of the poor is ever empty" (724) or

> I would not have it said of me that I merely "sounded the gong
> at Dodona". (483)

This last is a proverbial phrase for clattering, empty talk, like
Paul of Tarsus's phrase about "a sounding gong or a tinkling
cymbal." Sometimes it is hard to know whether a phrase is
traditional or of the poet's own coining, as with "The gods always
give little things to little men" (475) or "Our madness is worst at
its beginning" (480). A more extended example, which he has
certainly made his own, also shows Callimachus's pessimism:

> Anxieties press less heavily on a man,
>   and he is freed of a thirtieth part,
> when he bursts out with his troubles to a friend or companion,
>   or in the last resort to the unheeding winds. (714)

A thirtieth part seems a small riddance. But this is the poet who
wrote, with one of his favorite allusions, "Troilus wept less than
Priam" (491). The longer we live, the more we have to weep,
says the pessimist. "He whom the gods love dies young."

VI   *Lost Poetry*

The entry in *The Suda* says that Callimachus wrote poems in
every meter, and that the books, poetry and prose, written by
him number more than 800. *The Suda* does not attempt to give a
full list of these, but names a number of titles not otherwise
known. These include "The Coming of Io," "Semele," "Settlements of Argos," "Arcadia," "Glaucus," "Hopes." We must
assume that poems with these titles once existed, but they may
have been sections within *Aitia* or one of the other volumes of
which we are aware. *The Suda* also mentions satyric dramas,
tragedies, and comedies. Of these no trace remains. One epigram
(59) suggests some dramatic poetry, but the poet may merely be
donning a persona himself for epigrammatic purposes. But
another, a mock dedication of a mask by Agoranax, who won first
prize, suggests some displeasure, as if Callimachus himself were
defeated (49). A few titles survive from other sources, beyond
these and the poems we have treated elsewhere. It is not always
clear whether they refer to prose or poetical works, though
perhaps the work "On Athletic festivals" was in verse.

CHAPTER 7

Hymns

I Prototypes and Purpose

THE prototype of Callimachus's hymns, the one part of his corpus to survive more or less intact, is the Homeric hymn. In fact, we owe their survival to that fact, since they are preserved in an anthology of hymns by Homer, Callimachus, "Orpheus," and Proclus. The so-called Homeric hymns belong to an age of piety; we must not forget that, as in the hymn to Hermes, piety and playfulness are not incompatible. They are rooted in epic, and this gave them for Callimachus's day a curious combination of authority and archaism. Thirty-three or thirty-four of them are extant, and they must be only a small selection of such expressions of early ritual piety surviving certainly into the fifth century and perhaps later: some of these were undoubtedly in lyrical form but others, like those which went by the name of Homer, used the epic manner and had the dactylic hexameter as their medium. It is pertinent to add that, although the ascription of a corpus of hymns to Homer is found in Thucydides and other authorities, a certain body of opinion represented by one of the lives of Homer, was sceptical about the authorship: the hymn to Apollo is anciently ascribed to one Cynaethus, working about 500, which is odd, as internal evidence shows that it must be older. We can deduce that Alexandrian scholarship shared this scepticism from the fact that the commentators on Homer do not refer to the hymns. Callimachus was well aware of the attribution to Homer of poems which were not his: one of his epigrams (6) refers to this very subject. We can assume that he did not regard the hymns as by Homer, and this may well have influenced his acceptance of them as a model.

In fact, the longest of them, longer than Callimachus's longest, are as long as a book of *The Odyssey*, but each is of course self-contained. Callimachus had in fact a varied body of material as his basis. There was hieratic and deeply felt devotion in the hymn to Demeter, considerable charm in the hymn to Aphrodite, an aloof, numinous quality in the hymn to Apollo, unabashed humor in the hymn to Hermes, adventure in the hymn to Dionysus. It was just the raw material to appeal to his own sense of variety.

Callimachus, for all his debt to Euripides in other ways, was no rationalist of that school; the mood of his older contemporary Euhemerus, who saw the gods as idealized benefactors from the past, did not touch him; for all his pessimism he was not a doubter. Nor was he a poet to play with mere tradition; he valued tradition because it was related to reality; this is the whole point of his insistence on *Aitia*, on explanations and origins. The hymns are sincere expressions of religious devotion.

Their dates are uncertain, but it is fairly certain that their writing was spread over a number of years. G. Kaibel by an examination of the use of meter argued for the order 6, 3, 5, 1, 4, 2, but this cannot be taken as proved, and is not confirmed by such evidence as exists. We have some broad indications of date. Hymn 1 was probably not long after 283 BC; 2 was not written before the 250s, and might be as late as 247; 3 is totally uncertain in date. Hymn 4 cannot be before 270, but is not likely to be much later. No one even professes any evidence about 5. Hymn 6 belongs to the reign of Ptolemy II Philadelphus, and probably to his sole reign; that is, it is later than 283. It is likely that they are all later than 283, and that they cover in all a quarter of a century or more.

They were written for use in worship—though not all interpreters think so—but over-ingenious theories have been applied to their precise occasions. Hymn 2 was clearly written for the festival of Apollo Carneios at Cyrene. Ancient commentators link 5 with a festival of Pallas at Argos and 6 with a festival at Alexandria called the procession of the Basket, an imitation of the Athenian Thesmophoria. For the rest we are totally ignorant, but if three were written for particular festivals, we can be certain that the other three were not literary exercises, private devotional statements, or court poems dissociated from the context of worship.

Four of the hymns are in epic-Ionic, the last two in literary Doric, and we cannot help admiring Callimachus's command of both forms. His use of the hexameter is fluent and controlled. One well-known feature is his occasional use of a spondee instead of a dactyl in the fifth foot (as in 1, 5; 1, 7); it has the effect of giving the end of the line unusual weight, especially as it is usually employed with a single four-syllable word fitting the last two feet.[1] The device was taken up by Callimachus's Roman imitators, as by Catullus in his *Peleus and Thetis,* almost as the badge of their school, and won them the nickname of the *spondeiazontes.* Callimachus's style is rhetorical. He is, for example, continually using anaphora and rhetorical repetition of all kinds. In the second line of the first hymn Zeus is "ever mighty, ever Lord." Shortly after, four consecutive lines begin "Zeus . . . Zeus . . . Cretans . . . Cretans." Alliteration and assonance come in the same passage: PoTERoi, PaTER, EPseusanTo: "Which, Father, are fibbing?" He loves the evocative sound of proper names. "No other land," cries Delos, "will ever be so loved by a god,

> not Cerchnis by Poseidon, lord of Lechaeum,
> not Cyllene's hill by Hermes, not Crete by Zeus,
> as I by Apollo." (4, 271–3)

The more exotic the names the better, like the Arimaspi, Upis, Loxo, and happy Hecaerge (4, 292); if not, let them be simply unfamiliar, like Abantian Macris of the Ellopians, which is just Euboea (4, 20).

His primary source remains the Homeric hymn. This is modified by three other strands. One is Hesiod, who was for Callimachus a more compact and controlled writer, and at the same time a man of learning. A second is Pindar.[2] His hymns were lyrical, and Callimachus fed a strong lyrical impulse into all that he did. The third is Callimachus's own craft, wit, and flexibility.

No single view of the hymns is adequate. They were surely liturgical, but they were not merely liturgical. They were surely written for a variety of places, but they were also performed in Alexandria. They have considerable political reference, but they were not merely or even primarily political poems. There is an element of political allegory, but it is a mistake to press allegorical interpretations too hard, or to think that Zeus and

Apollo are merely the Ptolemies. There is also some assertion
and demonstration of literary values, but they are surely not
merely literary exercises or competitive entries. They are works
of complexity, and in that consists their fascination.[3]

II   *Hymn 1 to Zeus*

The first hymn is appropriately to the greatest of the gods,
Zeus. "Let us start from Zeus," wrote Callimachus's older
contemporary Aratus, and when Callimachus put his hymns
together that is where he started. The opening lines suggest an
actual festival:

> Zeus is receiving libations; what better theme
> for a hymn than the god, ever mighty, ever Lord,
> heaven's judiciary, victor over the Giants? (1–3)

This will have been in Alexandria, for the hymn later includes
flattery of the king. Now Ptolemy Philadelphus was exalted over
the heads of his older brothers,[4] and the hymn tells how Zeus was
exalted over the heads of his older brothers *on merit*. It is a
reasonable supposition therefore that it was written at a time
when Ptolemy's right to the throne was still being challenged. By
about 279 the brothers were all disposed of in different ways,
including murder. The most dangerous of them, Ptolemy
Ceraunos (the Thunderbolt), was at the height of his meteoric
career in about 281–280, and if we were to guess a date, that is
what it would be. It is a mistake to identify Ptolemy with Zeus: it
is also a mistake to ignore the political dimensions and miss the
double-talk.

The poet goes straight from his exordium to adjudicate
between two claimants for the honor of being Zeus's birthplace,
Crete and Arcadia. Callimachus settles it by a familiar proverb
(also quoted by Paul of Tarsus) such as he is fond of using:
"Cretans are ever liars." Then, with a brilliant pun, he says that
the Cretans *fabricated* a tomb for Zeus. There follows a
numinous description of the birthplace:

> In Parrhasia Rhea gave you birth, where a hill
> is strongly shrouded in thickets. The place there
> is holy; no creature that needs the birth-goddess,

>no woman sets foot there; the ancient Arcadians
>call it Rhea's primeval childbed. (10-4)

She needed water to wash away the stains of childbirth. But,
according to the myth, the rivers of Arcadia were not yet in
existence, and Callimachus lets his imagination play on the
thought in lines that were to give Ovid bitterly witty ideas about
describing the frozen rivers of south Russia:

>Iaon with its waves lifted numbers of oak trees
>high to the air, Melas supported wagons in plenty,
>scores of snakes established their nests above
>Carion for all its present water, walkers
>wandered over Crathis and pebbly Metope
>and went thirsty with all that water under foot. (22-7)

She struck the mountain, and water gushed out. She washed and
swaddled the baby and gave him to the river-nymph Neda to
carry off to Crete. There is an ambiguity, since a place named
Crete also existed in Arcadia. Neda receives her recompense—in
the main, as the poet punningly says. She meets Nereus, a witty
way of saying that the river flows into the sea.

Now follows in learned sonorous verse the familiar Cretan
legend:

>The nymph carrying you towards Cnossos was leaving
>Thenae, Father Zeus, (Thenae is near Cnossos),
>when suddenly, our God, your navel dropped off, and so
>the Cydonians in consequence call this the Navel Plain,
>Zeus, the companions of the Corybantes cradled you in their arms,
>the Ash-Nymphs of Dicte, and Adrasteia put you to sleep
>in a cot of gold, and you sucked the milky teat
>of the goat Amaltheia, and ate sweet honey as well.
>For all of a sudden the products of the Panacrian bee
>appeared on the mountains of Ida known as Panacon.
>The Curetes vigorously danced their war-dance around you,
>clashing their weapons, for the noise of the shields
>rather than your infant cries to reach Cronos's ears. (43-54)

Here is a laboriously brilliant double twist, since there was
another Thenae in Arcadia! Callimachus's scholarship is
unobtrusively accurate. There was another conflict of claims,

whether Zeus was brought up in a cave on Ida or Dicte. Archaeology tells us that the cult on Dicte was the older of the two, and Callimachus's reference to the ash-nymphs of Dicte shows that this was his view.

Zeus grew up, and we see another criterion of Callimachus's scholarship, internal plausibility.

> The poets of old failed to tell the whole truth.

He is speaking of Homer, Pindar, and others.

> They declared that the sons of Cronos drew lots for their three
> domains.
> Who would draw lots for Olympus or Hades—
> except a total fool? You toss up when the result
> does not matter: but these are poles apart.
> When I make up stories, I want them to persuade my hearers!
> (60-5)

It is delightfully down to earth. Zeus won sovereignty by action, by his power, by his merit. There follows the assertion that kings are Zeus's special concerns. Others he has left to lesser gods. They are his own. Callimachus quotes Hesiod: "Kings come from Zeus."[5] The reference to Hesiod is not just to secure a reputable theological authority; it is to show, as we have seen in *Aitia*, that Callimachus stands in a particular poetical tradition. But alongside this he is making a political point, almost the Divine Right of Kings. He makes explicit reference to

> our own sovereign, who has gone far beyond the rest.
> By evening he completes the tasks taken in hand in the morning,
> the major tasks by evening, the minor are done in the thinking.
> Other rulers take a year, or more, or find you frustrate
> their plans wholly and frustrate their ambitions. (86-90)

It is quite possible that Ceraunos was King of Thrace at this time.

So the hymn ends with a prayer and a piece of moderately worldly moralizing:

> Hail, Father, again hail; grant us goodness and success.
> Without goodness, riches cannot exalt men,
> nor goodness without prosperity. May you grant both! (94—6)

The formula of the prayer is religious and traditional, but the expansive comment is the poet's own, and, though the prayer is addressed to Zeus, kings come from Zeus, and what follows is written with a side-glance at Ptolemy.

III *Hymn 2 to Apollo*

The second hymn is of particular interest because of its association with Callimachus's birthplace, Cyrene. It is a very personal song, ending on a curiously personal note; yet it was surely written to be sung at Apollo's Dorian festival, the Carneia, in Cyrene. Between the lines we can discern the affection in which the poet held his home town. At the same time he was a court poet at Alexandria and could not give that affection open utterance in periods when Cyrene was out of favor: for example, this hymn could hardly belong to the period 250–247 when Egypt was at war with Cyrene. This is one clue to the date. The other is the reference to "my king" (26–7). From about 267–260 Ptolemy "the son" (whoever he was) was co-regent, and a plural would have been more natural. A likely date, then, would lie in the 250s. If we want to press the religio-political analogy (it is doubtful whether we should make it too precise), either Ptolemy I is equated with Zeus Soter and Philadelphus with his favorite son, or Philadelphus himself is regarded as a political Zeus and a cultural Apollo. But there is an alternative possibility. In 247 Ptolemy III succeeded to the throne and married Berenice, princess of Cyrene, and the two kingdoms were united. In this case Philadelphus has his analogue in Zeus (a strong equation in Theocritus) and Euergetes in his son. This would be a fitting date for such a song: it does not depend on the view which would further make it a mere political allegory, with Ptolemy as Apollo, Berenice as Cyrene, and Demetrius (whom she killed) as the lion. It is better to take the hymn at its face value, and to recognize the poet's extraordinary skill in offering more than one level of meaning to certain passages.

The hymn has a scenario. We are in Cyrene at the Carneia, waiting for the god's epiphany. The beginning is startlingly vivid:

> How Apollo's laurel bough quivers,
> his whole temple quivers! Back, back, you sinners!
> Phoebus is knocking at the door with shapely foot. (1–3)

There is here a sudden insight into everyday life. When you called on a neighbor, there was no doorbell or knocker; you would bang on the door with stick or foot.

> Don't you see? The palm from Delos gently swayed
> all of a sudden, the swan in the sky is melodiously chanting.
>
> (4-5)

It is an exquisite picture. The Delos palm has worried some interpreters; it was the celebrated palm on the island which supported Leto in her birth-pangs, and became the prey of souvenir-hunters: what is it doing in Cyrene? It is possible that the temple authorities had a shoot of the palm ceremonially transplanted, or that they had their own symbolic palm-tree in the temple precincts. But we do not need to believe more than that there were palm-trees about, as there undoubtedly were. They naturally become "Delian" in the god's presence, almost proleptically.

> And now the disciplined poet does a quite startling thing:
> Apollo's epiphany is not for all, but for the meritorious.
> To see him is to be exalted; to miss him is to be abased.
> Archer, we shall see you, and shall never be abased. (9-11)

These lines, which seem to presuppose an actual epiphany, are the kernel of the case for a political interpretation. But this is wrong: no one could say that Ptolemy moving in procession through the streets of Cyrene appeared only to the meritorious. Callimachus's faith that he will see the Archer-god is a mystical faith. It is an affirmation that he too is an ecstatic, an inspired poet.

The hymn gets under way. "The tortoise is at work again," says the poet wittily, referring to the lyre. The singers call for silence. The sea is silent. Thetis no longer keens for Achilles.

> Yes, the rock of tears postpones its grief,
> the streaming stone set firm in Phrygia,
> the marble like a woman open-mouthed in sorrow. (22-4)

This is Niobe, turned to stone in grief when Apollo killed her sons and Artemis her daughters. These three lines might be taken as representative of Callimachus—beautiful, allusive, relevant, an envisioned picture lifted out of the scholarly tomes of myth. All are silent to hear the cry, the familiar chant in the god's honor "Ië Paieon!" or, as we should read for reasons which will appear, "Hië Paieon!" Then an undoubtedly political touch follows.

> Cry "Hië! Hië!" It is not good to oppose the Blessed Ones.
> Anyone who fights the Blessed Ones would fight my king;
> any who fights my king, would fight Apollo too. (25-7)

This would fit either the late 250s when war between Cyrene and Egypt was threatening, or 247 in the uncertainties at the start of a new reign.

We return to Apollo, the golden Apollo, handsome and young, with perfumed hair. Here there is a touch of wit:

> Apollo's hair does not distil grease,
> but the power of healing. Any city in which those
> drops fall to the earth is protected from all danger. (39-41)

Panacea, the power of healing, is the name given to a number of plants. We go to Apollo's functions of patronage, for archers, singers, diviners and seers, and doctors whom he taught the lesson of deferring death.

Callimachus is now ready to go on to the mythology he is fascinated by. He takes off from Apollo's cult-title of Nomios, linked with the days when he pastured Admetus's animals.

> Quietly the herd of cattle would grow in number,
> the she-goats would not want for kids as Apollo
> watched the grazing, the ewes were milky and fertile,
> and all had lambs at their udders.
> The birth of one was quickly followed by its twin. (50-4)

Another of the god's functions follows, the patronage of town planning. He is described as "weaving" the foundations of cities. This anticipates an account of the *keraton* on Delos, an altar made entirely of goats' horns, "plaited" by the god himself; it was one of the tourist attractions of antiquity.

And now we see where this is leading. Callimachus too, inspired by the god, is a skillful weaver. One strand has been Apollo, the god of song, theme of this hymn sung at the Carneia

at Cyrene. Another has been Apollo, the city-god, who protects
the Ptolemies, whose healing power rests upon cities, who is
consulted about new foundations. A third has been his patronage
of divination and prophecy. A fourth has been his cult-titles. A
fifth has been his mythology. All these are woven together as
Callimachus embarks on the foundation myth of his home town:

> It was Phoebus too who told Battus of my fertile city,
> and as a raven, a good omen for the founder, led his people
> as they entered Africa, and swore that he would grant
> battlements to our kings. Apollo keeps his word.
> Apollo, many address you as the Helper,
> many as God of Claros; everywhere you have many names.
> I invoke you as Carneios; that's the tradition inherited.
>   (65-71)

He tells about the move from Sparta to Thera and Thera to
Africa, avoiding the name of Battus, stammerer, and calling the
founder instead "unfaltering Aristoteles"; he depicts the
sacrifice of bulls, the flowers on the altar, the perpetual fire, and
the dance. Callimachus with unobtrusive skill links the dance in
his own day both with a tradition of the pioneers dancing with
the women of Africa (who are described as "golden-haired";
red-headed girls are still to be seen in the land between the
Mediterranean and the desert), and with the earlier myth of the
nymph Cyrene:

> Our Lord saw them, and pointed them out to his bride
> as he stood on Myrtle Hill with its horns, when Hypseus's daughter
> killed the lion that was ravaging the cattle of Eurypylus.
> Apollo has never seen a dance more divine than that one;
> he has never granted any other city the advantage he gave Cyrene,
> remembering how he once ravished her. (90-5)

Myrtle Hill has been identified, with its horn-shaped rocks and
its myrtles still, southwest of Cyrene.
    The poet is not yet done. He produces still another *aition*, and
takes the hymn, which started by reminding us of the palm-tree
from Delos, to the god's other focal home at Delphi. He returns
to the cry "Hië! Paieon!" and derives it from the shouting people
of Delphi when Apollo kills the snake with his arrows. For "Hië,"

or something like it, means "Shoot!" "Hië! Hië! Paieon!" High let
the arrows fly!

Even this is not the end. Unexpectedly the poet confronts us
with his poetic creed:

> Envy whispered secretly in Apollo's ear:
> "I have no time for the poet whose songs are not as wide
> as the ocean's."
> Apollo kicked Envy aside and answered:
> "The flow of the river of Assyria is broad, but it carries down
> much flotsam and jetsam on its waters.
> The Melissae do not bring Deo water from any stream,
> only from the slender rivulet, pure and undefiled,
> which trickles, the pearl of waters from a holy spring."
> Hail, Lord! Send censure where Envy lives. (105—13)

It is a remarkable conclusion. We may notice one brilliant touch.
The wheel of the poem comes full circle. Apollo's foot, which at
the beginning gives a welcome to the faithful, now removes the
unworthy. The scholiast comments, "In these words he rebukes
those who taunted him with inability to write a long poem, a gibe
which constrained him to write *Hecale.*" Callimachus makes a
parable of this: his answer, with memorable illustrations, is that
"Small is Beautiful" in literature, in religion, and in life. But there
is an explicit rebuke to envy or malice of any kind: it deserves
censure. Such a conclusion may seem inappropriate for a hymn
on a public occasion. Not really. The odes of Pindar have
personal allusions in the same way. Callimachus stands in a
tradition. The lyric impulse in this hymn is strong; we can be
fairly certain of a debt to a lost hymn of Alcaeus. The poet is the
servant of Apollo: the words are appropriate. He is justifying the
writing of a hymn, and quite a short one, and his hearers no doubt
applauded that; they may have realized that implicit too was the
praise of a polis such as Cyrene, and the sense that a cosmopolis
such as Alexandria does not offer the only way of life.

IV   *Hymn 3 to Artemis*

K. J. McKay called his celebrated study of the fifth hymn "The
Poet at Play." That same mood is strong in the third hymn. It
begins, as usual, directly:

Artemis (it is a serious matter for poets to forget her)
is our theme. Her care includes the bow, hunting the hare,
the wide-ranging dance, sport on the mountains. (1-3)

Then follows one of the most charming vignettes in Greek
literature. Artemis is depicted as a little girl climbing on Zeus's
knee and asking him for presents:

"Daddy, let me keep my maidenhood for ever,
and give me many names, so that Phoebus mayn't brag over me.
And give me a bow and arrows—hold on, father I'm not asking you
for a quiver or a big bow. The Cyclopes will readily
make me arrows and a bow I can bend." (6-10)

The requests pile up. The little voice goes remorselessly on and
on. She's going to be Bringer of Light, wear a tunic, kill wild
animals, have a choir of her own, have gods to do the chores, the
little aristocrat.

Give me twenty nymphs of Amnisus to wait on me,
to look after my hunting-boots, and when I'm tired of shooting
the lynx or stag, to groom my swift hounds.
And give me all the mountains. For city let me have
whichever you like. Artemis won't often be going down to town.
                                                      (15-9)

Her only visits will be to help women in childbirth. Then there is
an entertaining picture of the little girl trying to touch Zeus's
beard to confirm her requests, and unable to reach. Zeus is
delighted, and says, with an admirable touch of realism:

"When goddesses bear me children
like this, I scarcely need to bother about
Hera's jealous tempers." (29-31)

He promises her all she asks for and more. The poet succeeds by
a variety of devices in working in a surprising number of the
goddess's titles and functions.

The little girl flies off; we have a vivid impression of a bundle
of energy. She first picks out her choir of sixty nine-year-old
nymphs, daughters of Oceanus. Then they all go off to see the
monstrous Cyclopes who, says the poet in a weighty four-word
line, were "manufacturing Poseidon a horse-trough." The panic

of the girls, except for Artemis, is well conveyed through the horror-movie scene.

> The nymphs were scared when they saw the fearsome monsters
> looking like the cliffs of Ossa—all below their brow
> had a single eye, the size of a quadruple shield,
> glaring out balefully—and when they heard the clang
> of the loudly ringing anvil and the colossal blast
> of the bellows and the Cyclopes' heavy panting. Etna shrieked,
> Trinacia, home of the Sicans, shrieked, Italy nearby
> shrieked, Cyrnus came in with a great scream,
> when they raised their hammers over their shoulders
> and with a mighty effort took turns in striking
> the bronze as it bubbled from the furnace, or the iron.
>
> (51-61)

No shame to them (*ou nemesis,*a famous Homeric phrase). Even in Olympian families mothers threaten naughty girls with the Cyclopes, and Hermes covers himself with ash and pretends to be one, and the girls hide their faces in their hands and rush to their mothers. It is an insight into Greek family life projected onto Olympus. But Artemis showed no timidity. She'd been there before at the age of three, sat on one of the monster's laps, and pulled at the hairs on his chest.

She makes her request, and scuds off to Pan to get some hounds from him. He gives her thirteen—there is no significance in the total number. They are carefully envisaged but we cannot be certain of the details. Two are black-and-white: the Greek may mean half-black or half-white, but it makes no difference. With the next three the reading is uncertain: the manuscripts would give them hanging ears, like spaniels, which may be right; other suggestions are "reddish" or, perhaps most likely, "Molossian," the most famous of all ancient hounds. Then comes what we would call a Dalmatian, with spots. Finally, seven bitches from Laconia,

>   exceedingly fast
> on the track of deer and the wide-eyed hare,
> quick to uncover the stag's lair and the porcupine's
> burrow, and to pick up the antelope's trail. (94-7)

So off she goes with her pack, and sees five huge golden-horned deer playing together, and thinks—she is delightfully spontaneous—what a marvellous first "bag" they would make. She has no weapons yet; she does not use hounds; but she secures four of them alive and yokes them to her car. The fifth escapes to provide a Labor for Heracles; it is wholly characteristic of the poet to link different strands of myth in this way.

Callimachus in this hymn continually renews his impulse with a fresh invocation to Artemis, bringing in more of her titles, and by rhetorical questions, which he answers himself, introducing further aspects of the myth. There is one slight curiosity. Within the space of ten lines he describes her weapons as of gold, and asks the question "How often, goddess, did you experiment with the silver bow?" (119) His answer is that she started with trees, then animals, and turned to human evil-doers. These she punishes, and the poet uses a daring expression for the form of the punishment, "Disease grazes on their cattle" (125), a notable inversion. Those she favors prosper:

> They do not pass
> to the graveyard except to escort the elderly there. (131-2)

In homes she blesses, sisters-in-law and brothers' wives draw up their chairs to a single table: again we get an insight, this time into some of the tensions of family life.

> Lady, may all true friends of mine be of their number,
> may I too, Queen, and poetry always be my life. (136-7)

That is a sincere prayer.

Now he pictures the goddess arriving at Olympus with some trophy of the chase. Apollo used to receive this, but now Heracles has upstaged him. Heracles is portrayed with as consuming a paunch as ever in Aristophanes, and here the gods, even his mother-in-law (Hera), laugh at him, as they laugh at Hephaestus in Homer: we must remind ourselves that the Greeks did not find such laughter incompatible with religious devotion. Heracles tries to persuade Artemis to concentrate on large game; his excuse is the harm they do to men.

> "Shoot at dangerous animals; then men will call you
> their helper, as they do me. Leave deer and hares
> to graze the hills. What harm could deer or hares

> do? It's boars which destroy farmland, boars destroy
>   crops.
> And cattle do men a lot of harm. Shoot them as well."
>   (153-7)

It is very funny. Artemis leaves her nymphs to groom the deer, and goes in. All the gods say "Come and sit by me!" It is again a vivid picture of a mixed dinner party when an exceptionally attractive girl enters. But she goes over to her brother Apollo.

A slightly intrusive paragraph identifies allusively some of her shrines in Delos, Laconia, and Attica, with reference to the legend that she was worshiped with human sacrifice among the Tauri of the Crimea, and that the cult, shorn of its excesses, was brought to Brauron in Attica by Iphigeneia. The poet prays that his oxen may never be at work when her nymphs are dancing at these homes of hers, or they would have limping steps and drooping necks on their return because the Sun-god has to stop and watch the dance, and that lengthens the day. This is an over-ingenious conceit.

The questions recur.

> Which of the islands, what mountain gives you most pleasure?
> Which harbor? What city? Which of the nymphs do you love
> more than the others? What heroines do you have in your train?
> Tell me, goddess. You tell me, and I'll make a poem of it for
>   others.
> Among islands Doliche is your favorite, among cities Perge,
> among mountains Taÿgetus, among harbors the Euripus. (183-8)

The Euripus is the strait between Euboea and the mainland: the harbor is Aulis, where the Greek flèet assembled against Troy. Taÿgetus is the mountain that dominates Sparta. Perge is in Pamphylia, on the south coast of Turkey. Curiously, we cannot identify Doliche. The *Etymologicum Magnum* makes it Euboea, Stephanus of Byzantium says it is Icarus in one entry, but in another finds it an island off the coast of Lycia.

Her favorite nymph is Britomartis, and Callimachus tells the story of how King Minos fell madly in love with her and pursued her over peak and precipice for nine months. He almost caught her but she leapt from a cliff into the sea and was saved by some fisherman's nets. This is an *aition* of the names Dictyna (Our

Lady of Nets) and Dictaeon (Net-hill). The refusal to touch
myrtle in the ritual for Dictyna is explained by the fact that a
bough of myrtle caught in her dress and hindered her escape.
Britomartis, as Callimachus says, is a kind of doublet of the
goddess. The poet goes on to her other favorites. Cyrene he has
to bring in, and adds Paris, and Odysseus's mother Anticlea.

> These were the first women to wear on their shoulders
> > stout bows
> and quivers for their arrows. The strap went over their
> > right
> shoulder; the breast was always visibly naked. (212-4)

Callimachus is full of such visual pictures. He goes on to Atalanta
and the boar-hunt at Calydon, the tusks still, he says, on view in
Arcadia. Then, with grim humor, of two Centaurs she shot for
insolence:

> And I have a strong suspicion that Hylaeus and that stupid
> > Rhoecus
> for all their hatred cannot criticize her archery,
> in Hades. (222-4)

Skillfully the poet works his way towards the great temple of
Ephesus, one of the Seven Wonders of the World. He takes us to
Miletus and Samos, gives her a title "Throned-on-high" from
Ephesus, speaks, with a blatant pun between shrine and ship (in
Greek very close), of Agamemnon's offering before he crossed to
Asia Minor. Then an allusion to the way the goddess saved from
madness the daughters of the king of Argos leads to that other
company of women dedicated to her, the Amazons who set up at
Ephesus a statue under an oak tree, and danced a war-dance
around it. Around this statue the temple was founded, a splendid
spectacle. Callimachus tells evocatively how Lygdamis and the
Cimmerians from the far north tried to rase it.

> Wretched monarch, his sin was great. There was to be
> no journey back to Scythia for him or any other
> of all those whose wagons stood in the fields
> of Caÿster. Your arrows are Ephesus's permanent defense.
> > (255-8)

So come final titles and final warnings (allowing for more mythological examples). None should dishonor Artemis: witness Oeneus. None should challenge her archery: witness Agamemnon. None should seek to take her virginity: witness Otus or Orion. None should miss her dance: witness Hippo (Hippolyte).

> Hail, great Sovereign, look graciously on my song. (268)

It is not a wholly satisfactory poem. Callimachus had tried to do and to include too much: his effects are sometimes forced, the piling-on is too intense. Yet it is a poem of quite extraordinary skill in the variety and ingenuity of its effects, the controlled variations of pace, the humor and occasional grimness, the visual pictures, and above all the charm of its genre portrayal of the little girl at the outset.

V *Hymn 4 to Delos*

The fourth is the longest and most elaborate of the hymns, extending to 326 lines. There is a definite point of political reference, when the unborn Apollo prophesies the birth of another god in Cos, Ptolemy II Philadelphus, and his victory over the Celts. It lasts only some twenty-five lines (165-90), carefully placed in the poem, and is to be treated as a flattering adjunct, not as the point of the poem. The poem is about Delos, and the most likely occasion for performance would have been the Delian festival, though we may reasonably postulate a court performance at Alexandria, either beforehand (offering the opportunity, like the official "recitations" in Imperial Rome, for unobtrusive censorship) or afterwards. We should remember that since 308 there had existed a League of the Islanders with headquarters at Delos under the protectorate of Egypt.

The reference to the invasion of Greece by the Gauls gives us a *terminus a quo* for the hymn in 278. We can lower this to 270, since we know that Ptolemy was not deified before 270, and he is explicitly called a god (165). There are other clues to the date. The account of Ptolemy's far-extending sway is paralleled by a more detailed account in Theocritus (17, 86-92). This was certainly written before the death of Arsinoe in 270; the great German scholar Wilamowitz argued for its appearance in the

context of the first Syrian War (274–271). Callimachus's hymn
and Theocritus's idyll are unlikely to be widely separated in
date. The extent of the dominion would fit well a date around
270, when it included substantial parts of Palestine and Asia
Minor as well as Cyprus and the Cyclades.

The scholiast associates the danger from the Celts, not merely
with the invasion itself, but with the mutiny of Gallic mercen-
aries whom Ptolemy had subsequently enlisted.[6] This would fit a
date in 270 or 269.

The hymn starts with a question, or rather with a double
question.

Well, my soul, what's the occasion to be? When will you hymn the holy
island of Delos, Apollo's nurse? (1–2)

Apollo requires poets to sing of Delos. So we have a logical
succession of hymns. After Zeus, the poet honors in turn Apollo,
Artemis, and the island that gave both birth—though it is slightly
odd that Artemis receives no mention in the narrative. As the
poet turns to a description of the island, it is hard to realize that
he had never been there:

> She's wind-blown and forbidding and wave-beaten,
> fitter course for gulls than for horses,
> set firm in the sea, which rolls around her in its fullness,
> dropping plenty of spindrift from the waters of Icarus.
>   (11–5)

Yet the other islands are happy to concede her eminence:
Callimachus picks them out allusively: Corsica ("Phoenician
Cyrnus"), Euboea ("Abantian Macris of the Ellopians"), Sardinia
("Desirable Sardo"), Cyprus ("The island to which Cypris
swam"). But they depend on the protection of walls and towers:
Delos's protection is Apollo.

Callimachus proceeds to the legends of Delos, which he tells
winningly. Delos was once a floating island, known as Asterie.
Her wanderings are wittily recounted: sailors coasting the
isthmus would spot her, but by the time they set out again she'd
vanished. Asterie passed from insignificance (*a-delos*, a pun) to

glory by standing up to Hera's anger with Leto. Hera set Ares to watch the mainland and Iris to watch the islands, and to threaten any city which might offer Leto a place to bear the child. One is tempted to say that there was no room in the inn. What follows, even allowing for the personification of places as nymphs, river gods, and the like, is a witty conceit:

> Arcadia fled, Auge's holy hill Parthenion
> fled, old Pheneius followed and fled,
> the whole land of Pelops which depends on the Isthmus fled.
> (70-2)

The anaphora is one of Callimachus's favorite rhetorical effects. Some of the refugees are more firmly delineated; the streams, Dirce and Strophie, as little girls fearfully clutching the hands of the great river god Ismenus (whose black pebbles, a visual picture, also symbolize doom); another river god Asopus, limping at the knee, crippled by a thunderbolt; the ash-nymph checking her dance, whirling around and turning pale with fear not for herself but for her comrade the oak tossing in the angry storm. This picture draws from Callimachus one of those engaging asides which makes his passion for learning intensely personal.

> Tell me, Muses, my own goddesses,
> were the oaks really coeval with the nymphs?
> The nymphs laugh when rain helps the oaks to grow,
> The nymphs cry when the oaks shed their leaves. (87-5)

It is a charming picture, clarified by a touch of rhetoric.

Apollo, still unborn, is furious—his anger is conveyed in a multiplicity of m-sounds (89)—and prophesies before his time in a concatenation of t-sounds against Thebe, the eponymous nymph of Thebes, foretelling the fate of Niobe ("a loud-mouthed woman") who boasted her twelve children against Leto's two, only to see Apollo and Artemis shoot her twelve down. Apollo renounces Thebes: "I am pure and must have pure protectors." So Leto turns to Achaea, and then to Thessaly.

There follows the finest episode of the poem. The river Peneius flees at Leto's approach. Leto calls him back in words both pathetic and amusing:

> "Phthiotian Peneius, why are you now challenging the
> winds?
> Father, you're not riding a racehorse, you know!" (112-3)

When he won't listen, she is near desperation:

> "My precious burden,
> where am I to carry you? My leg muscles are worn out with
> weariness." (116-7)

She calls on Mt. Pelion, where in a line of untranslatable, majestic
sonority "lionesses find relief from-the-birth-pangs of-their-
rough-brood." "Rough" is brilliant: it means both savage and
shapeless. This last cry moves the river god:

> Then Peneius answered her with tears in his eyes:
> "Leto, Necessity is a great goddess. It's not my will
> to repudiate your pains, my lady. I'm familiar with
> others
> cleansed from childbirth in my water. It's Hera
> with her dreadful threats. Look up, at the sentinel
> keeping watch on the mountain-top; he would happily
> rip me up from the roots."

It is reminiscent of a terrifying canvas by Goya.

> "What can I do? Do you really want
> Peneius to perish? 'Let the day of destiny come!
> For your sake I will dare all, even if I have to wander
> with stream sucked thirstily down to eternity
> and alone among rivers to be in utter disgrace.
> Here I am. What more do you want? Just call in Eilithyia.' " (120-32)

It is a heroic defiance. The response is spectacular:

> Ares
> was on the point of lifting up the crags of Pangaeum from
> their foundations
> and tossing them into his swirling waters and obliterating
> his streams.

In the sky he thundered, and beat his shield with the
point
of his spear, and it rang out as for war. The heights of Ossa
and the plain of Crannon and the gale-torn foothills
of Pindus shook, and all Thessaly danced
with fear at the mighty sound which thundered from his
shield (133–40)

Peneius stands his ground, but Leto will not have his self-
sacrifice and tells him to save himself.

Leto limps wearily to the islands. They too disown her. The
unborn Apollo will not let her halt at Cos: this is destined to be
the birthplace of another god—Ptolemy. The passage of court
flattery follows. Ptolemy shall realize his father's character. The
Gauls are described as latter-day Titans, flurrying down like
snowflakes, in number as the stars of the Milky Way. The
devastation they spread is conveyed as a present experience.
The prophetic voice says that the hated shields of which they are
so proud "shall bring the foolish tribe of Galatians a journey of
death." One wonders whether the Greek-speaking Jew, Paul of
Tarsus, had this passage in mind when he called his correspon-
dents "foolish Galatians" because they were proffered the Word
of Life and preferred the way of death.[7]

The precocious baby now draws his mother's attention to the
floating island of Asterie, drifting on the waves "like an asphodel
flower". Asterie, like Peneius, defies Hera, and calls Leto over.
Leto comes, unfastens her belt, leans her shoulders against the
famous palm-tree, crushed by helplessness and pain, with sweat
pouring like rain down her body, and calls on her son to be born
in an astonishing, panting, ambiguous line with a suggestion of
epiphany, "Be born, be born, my son, and come kindly come from
your mother's womb" (214). It is curious that there is here no
reference to Artemis. In some versions she was born first and
helped her mother in Apollo's birth; here there is not even an
inkling of a twin. Callimachus, a good storyteller, keeps up the
suspense, even though we know the outcome. The scene
switches to Hera. Iris, the faithful messenger, rushes up
somewhat out of breath, somewhat fearfully, with the news. She

calls Asterie "the scum of the sea" (225) and settles at Hera's feet, in the poet's whimsical picture, like a hunting bitch, ears pricked up even in sleep. Hera is naturally angry and curses all Zeus's mistresses:

> "You abominations of Zeus, may you now like this all marry covertly and bear clandestine children, not even where poor mill-girls wrestle with difficult births, but where the seals of the sea pup, among solitary reefs." (240–3)

But she is not angry with Asterie, because Asterie had rejected Zeus's approaches.

Now we are ready for the birth. The sacred swans sing seven songs (this is used as an *aition* of the seven strings of the lyre), the foundations of Delos turn to gold, in a combination of visual imagery and rhetorical effect:

> At that moment, Delos, all your foundations were changed to
>   gold,
> the wheel-lake flowed all day long with gold,
> your native olive tree showed leaves of gold,
> the deep, meandering waters of Inopus flooded with gold. (260–3)

The nymph Asterie-Delos takes up the child. Her speech has been called the Magnificat of Delos. She describes herself as "not yielding to the plough" (268); it is a description of her rocky terrain, but it alludes, in a common metaphor, to her refusal to yield to Zeus. No other land will receive such love as Delos will receive from Apollo, she says, and she will be able to stop being a tramp: there is a subtle ambiguity here, as she acts as wet-nurse to the child.

Callimachus characteristically begins to round off his poem by drawing in other points of reference: the freedom of Delos from war and death (no one was buried there); the tithes offered, and the contests of choirs; the traditions of the Hyperboreans, the people from the remote north ("beyond the North Wind") sending their offerings, and the dedication of the hair of girls and the first beard of boys to their remote ancestors; the incense and the dancing; the traditional song from Lycia; the archaic statue of Aphrodite (set up by Theseus after his escape from the labyrinth and the Minotaur in Crete); the annual visit of the state galley from Athens (such a visit, a time of holiness, caused the postponement of Socrates's execution); the customary acts of pilgrims, raining blows on the altar and sinking their teeth into the sacred olive with hands tied behind their backs (the poet offers an *aition* that these were games invented by Asterie-Delos to entertain young Apollo). No sailor, however urgently pressed, would dream of sailing past Delos without landing to share in these acts.

> Joyous center of the islands, hail to you,
> hail to Apollo and to Leto whom he delivered. (325-6)

So Callimachus saves to the end his climactic touch: the god of healing was his own precocious midwife.

The thread of narrative with its skillfully varied pace gives this hymn particular coherence and interest. The descriptive writing is vivid and evocative, and there are powerful touches of characterization. It has whimsicality, too, which we should not miss. None of this detracts from the religious devotion or the unity of the whole.

VI   *Hymn 5 The Bath of Pallas*

The fifth hymn is one of only two in the Dorian dialect (some epic forms are preserved) and is the only one to use elegiac couplets. Elegiac threnody has Doric associations which would make this appropriate to Argos. It has no discernible point of courtly reference, and some critics have supposed for this reason that it antedates the poet's introduction to the court. Ostensibly it relates to a festival at Argos. There was a temple there dedicated to Athene Oxyderces (Sharp-Eyed). By tradition the temple was established by Diomedes, and contained two objects of great sanctity, the Palladium, an image of Athene stolen from Troy by Odysseus and Diomedes, and Diomedes' own shield.[8] These objects, the scholiast tells us, were taken from the temple annually and ritually bathed in the river Inachus. Such rituals were common in antiquity; the Athenian Plynteria is only one example among many; and to this day in some parts of Italy the image of the Virgin Mary is treated in the same way. Nothing in the hymn is incompatible with its use at such a ritual, and despite

the scepticism of some interpreters it is likely that it was
specially written for performance at the festival.

The hymn begins with vigor and directness:

> All attendants on Pallas at her bath, come out
> come out! The sacred steeds
> are whinnying. I hear them. The goddess is dressed
> for the journey.
> quick, quick, golden-haired daughters of Pelasgus!
> (1–4)

"Come" or "come out" is a repeated motif, a formal processional
term directed first to the girls, then to the goddess. We are told
how Athene always cared for her horses (suggesting that horse-
grooming is part of the ritual), then how she never used
elaborate perfumes or unguents: this is an *aition* for the simple
olive oil naturally used on the wooden statue. She never used a
mirror either, even for the Judgment of Paris: an entertaining
vignette, by contrast, shows Aphrodite preening herself before a
mirror, adjusting and readjusting a single curl.

The poet turns to call Athene to come out. The first call is
followed by an account of how the legendary priest Eumedes,
threatened with lynching, took the holy image with him

> and went to live on Mount Creion,
> yes, Mount Creion, and, goddess, set you up on those
> broken crags
> named the Heights of Pallas. (40–2)

The second call is followed by a warning that this is a holy day,
and those who seek water must draw it from the springs, not the
river. The warning is repeated three times with a different verb.

> For Inachus will come down from the mountain pastures,
> with golden flowers in his waters,
> bringing Athene a worthy bath. (49–51)

But a second warning follows. No one except her attendants may
see the goddess naked. The bathing of the image is a Mystery.
The warning forms a bridge to the main myth.

The poet calls the goddess a third time. While waiting he will
tell the attendants a story. Once upon a time there was a nymph

deeply loved by Athene. Her name, Chariclo, is held up for a
dozen lines, but we are told, significantly, that she was Teiresias's
mother. Teiresias was the famous blind prophet of Thebes, who
plays an importance rôle in Sophocles' *Antigone* and *King
Oedipus* and in Euripides's *The Bacchae*. Chariclo shared in
everything with Athene.

> It happened that the two of them disrobed
> by the beautiful stream of the Spring of the Horse on Helicon,
> and bathed. The peace of noon gripped the mountain.
> They both bathed. The hour was midday.
> Unbroken peace gripped the mountain. (70–4)

It is a daring piece of repetitive writing. There is a sinister
undercurrent, the calm before a storm, for midday is a dangerous
hour for divine encounter.

> Teiresias, with his jowl just darkening, was sweeping with his
> > hounds
> over the holy hill, an only child. (75–6)

In his thirst he went to the spring for a drink, unintentionally saw
the goddess naked, and lost his sight. The goddess was angry, yet
spoke in pity, and the poet creates the tone of pity by starting her
words with the gentler pentameter. But night took the boy's eyes
from him.

> He stood speechless. Pain riveted his knees.
> Helplessness checked his voice. (83–4)

His mother was frantic: "Is that how goddesses show their
friendship?" She transfers her anger to the mountain, and says in
a bitter pun that it has lost a few *dorkas* (roe-deer, named from
its large eyes) and taken her child's eyes. She threw her arms
around her son, lamenting like the nightingale. Athene's answer
was of divine calm. She did not will the boy's blindness: it was
inexorable divine law. Teiresias's act was involuntary: so is
Athene's punishment of him. But Actaeon's parents would pray
to see their son blind. His requital for accidentally coming on
Artemis at her bath was to be a meal for his own hounds: there is
a grim sick Waughish humor in the account. Instead Teiresias
shall enjoy the privileges of a prophet: he shall understand birds;

he shall deliver oracles; he shall have a staff to guide his steps; he shall have long life; and he shall uniquely have the reputation for wisdom among the dead. The lines recounting the privileges of Teiresias carefully balance the lines telling of Chariclo's earlier joys. The Sharp-Eyed goddess may deprive the boy of his sight, but she grants him inner vision. It is interesting that Callimachus makes nothing of the legend of Teiresias experiencing a twofold sexuality, the "old man with wrinkled dugs".[9]

> Now Athene is actually coming. Welcome the goddess,
>   you girls whose duty it is,
> with words of piety and prayers and praises.
>   Hail, goddess! Protect Inachus's Argos. (137-40)

The epiphany, in the second hymn for only the poet and a few others, is here for all.

VII   Hymn 6 to Demeter

The festival which is the *mise-en-scène* of the sixth hymn is the Thesmophoria in honor of Demeter. The day of fasting is over: it is now the procession of the Sacred Basket *(Kalathos)*. But the hymn is not timed to fit in with a procession: it is a general contribution. The locale is not unambiguously stated. Ancient commentators, who may be guessing, but are guessing on the basis of more evidence than we possess, say Alexandria, and add that Ptolemy Philadelphus had introduced the festival; no doubt Callimachus is describing what he has seen there. Other interpreters have argued for Cnidos, where Triopas was worshipped as a hero, or Cyrene, partly on grounds of certain dialectal forms, partly because of the reference to "the Black men and the home of the golden apples" (11) which fits Cyrene. This ambiguity has led some interpreters to deny its liturgical use. But the Thesmophoria was widely celebrated, and the poet might well wish to write a hymn which could be used in more than one place.

The dialect, as in the fifth hymn, is a modified literary Doric. K. J. McKay in a monumentally provocative study has seen it as standing in the line of the Dorian comedy of Epicharmus and others, and has emphasized Callimachus's mischievousness and even flippancy. McKay has thrown light on many passages, and he is right to see a comic element in the poem, but not to exaggerate it at the expense of other facets; indeed in the details of his minute inspection one feels he is sometimes, in the cliché (appropriate to this poem), failing to see the wood for the trees.

The shape of the hymn is not unlike that of the other Doric hymn, the fifth. They are almost identical in length, though differently proportioned. Both begin with a liturgical setting. Both move to a myth in which the parent is a favorite of the goddess, the son commits an offense and is punished for it, and the parent protests. Both expatiate on the benefits brought by the goddess. Both return to the liturgical setting.

As usual, the poet plunges straight in:

> The Holy Basket is coming, women, raise your voices:
> "All hail, Demeter, rich in nurture, rich in grain!" (1-2)

We move quickly with some alliteration (10) to the picture of Demeter as the *mater dolorosa* traveling the world over, not once but three times (this and other variants may come from a lost poem by Philitas) in search of her ravished daughter, without drinking, without eating, without washing. Then the poet breaks off to fit in the statutory words of praise:

> No, no, let us not speak of the events which brought tears
>   to Deo.
> Better to tell how she gave cities ordinances to their
>   satisfaction.
> Better to tell how she was the first to cut straw and
> sacred cornsheaves and set oxen to tread them,
> at the time when she taught Triptolemus that admirable skill.
>   (17-21)

"Better to tell how—as a warning against offenses"—and the next line is frustratingly missing, but it is a bridge to the myth.

Demeter had a sacred grove in Thessaly: the description owes something to the enchanted woodlands of *The Odyssey;* it is watered by a stream ambiguously described as *alektrinon,* of silvery sheen but also of amber. The prince of the house of Triopas, Erysichthon, takes twenty giant attendants to put axes to this grove. Erysichthon is the name of a Giant on the Altar of Zeus at Pergamum, and McKay has rightly suggested that the prince is here portrayed as a giant himself. They start on a poplar, as tall as the sky, where the nymphs like to play: the manuscript reading is "on which," and McKay may be right in suggesting that the shimmering of the leaves is the nymphs at play. The poplar-nymphs are the Heliades, Daughters of the Sun, whose tears drop amber: *alektrinon* has prepared us for this. This poplar first feels the axe and screams a warning to the rest: the poet has again prepared us for the personification. Demeter hears, and comes disguised as her own priestess to warn the prince: McKay is oversubtle in suggesting that her words are designed to emphasize the generation gap and provoke the young men. Callimachus is a Euripidean, and he is deliberately recalling the scene in *The Bacchae* where the god Dionysus gives his human antagonist Pentheus a last chance. Erysichthon's response is violent. He glares at her like a lioness with cubs disturbed by a hunter and cries "Out of the way, before I plant my axe in your body." He is going to build a dining-hall, and, we may add, being a giant needs a sky-high poplar to support the roof. Demeter now appears as her true self, towering, like her poplar, to the sky. The attendants rush away, leaving their axes still in the trees. She lets them go—they were only obeying orders—and turns to their master.

> "Yes, yes, build your house, you cur, you cur, and hold
> your feasts. You'll have plenty of them in the future."
> (63-4)

Now Erysichthon is under a curse: it is poetic justice, since he was intending to build a dining-hall:

> Without more delay she filled him with an intolerable
>   devouring hunger,
> blazing, powerful. (66-7)

Blazing, Aithon, is another name for Erysichthon, and the poet is again preparing a point. However much the giant eats, he is still hungry. His parents are ashamed and his mother has to make excuses in refusing invitations on his behalf: he's debt-collecting, or traveling abroad, or checking the sheep on the mountain, or else (covering up for tears in which grief and resentment are ambiguously mixed) he's been gored by a boar, or hit by a discus, or thrown from a horse. Meantime, pouring food into Erysichthon is like pouring it into the bottom of the sea. At the same time he is wasting away like snow on the hills or a wax doll in the sun (used as a surrogate in curses, but he is no surrogate). His mother, his two sisters, his wet-nurse, and his ten maidservants are in tears. His father Triopas would call on Poseidon (who paid no attention) and say "You're no father of mine." Here is a touch of Euripidean realism, for there were plenty of other genealogies for Triopas, and Callimachus is showing his scholarship by preferring one of the others.

> "I could wish that he'd been
> shot down by Apollo and laid out for burial with my own hands.
> Now he's sitting, damned Starvation in person, before my eyes.
> Free him from his foul disease—or else take him
> and feed him yourself."   (100–4)

This is witty. First the effort of laying out the giant; then the carefully prepared identification of Erysichthon with Starvation; then the desperate handing over of responsibility to the god. The boy has eaten all the sheep, the cattle, the mules, the heifer his mother was fattening for Hestia (the poet is playing with a proverbial expression for desperate action), the champion racehorse, the warhorse, and Whitetail, the bogey of the mice. He literally has eaten his father out of house and home, and at last the thing is out in the open and he sits at the crossroads begging for the garbage from others' meals (an echo of *The Odyssey* here). And now Callimachus does not complete the story, either with the cannibalism found in some versions or with Erysichthon's death. He breaks off:

> Demeter, I pray never to have friends or neighbors
> you hate. I hate bad neighbors.   (116–7)

There is a reference to Aeschylus's *Agamemnon* 1004 where the "neighbor" is Disease.

We return to the procession:

> Maidens, sing; mothers, add your voices:
> "All hail, Demeter, rich in nurture, rich in grain!" (118—9)

What follows is both a prayer and a promise. Four white horses
pull the wagon with the Basket: so Demeter will bring a white
(i.e., favorable) spring, summer, autumn, and winter. The
procession walks barefoot: so their heads and feet will be kept
free from evil. Then

> As the casket-carriers bear caskets full of gold,
> so may we enjoy gold in plenty. (126—7)

The casket (*liknon*) is filled with the gold of harvest. So comes
the final prayer, in which the point of the myth is taken up in all
piety:

> Hail, goddess. Keep this city safe, in unity
> and prosperity. Give us in the fields ripe crops.
> Feed our cattle, bring apples, corn-ears, harvest.
> Feed Peace too, that a man may reap as he ploughs.
> Be gracious to me: I pray three times to you, mighty Queen of
> Goddesses. (134—8)

The threefold prayer at the end parallels the threefold circuit of
the world at the beginning.

The hymn to Demeter is the wittiest and (it is not wrong to
say) the funniest of the hymns. But it is a mistake to interpret it as
mere wit. Callimachus has a respect for myth. More, he has a
respect for religious festivals. And it is within this context that
we may read—and enjoy—the wit.

VIII   *Conclusion*

The *Hymns* are the one extensive survival from Callimachus's
corpus. Callimachus's is a complex genius. He can bring together
wit and pathos, beauty and horror, past myth and present life,
demonstrative learning and unobtrusively contrived simplicity,
all in the context of religion. This was natural in the ancient
world where religion was as large as life. The audience that
laughed at Dionysus in *The Frogs* (a god receiving a schoolboy's
whacking!) and shuddered at Dionysus in *The Bacchae* believed
in Dionysus: they laughed at him, shuddered at him, and adored
him. It was not very different a hundred and fifty years later.
Callimachus has a reverence for religion as he has a respect for

myth: he wants to get it right. He brings to the hymn, traditionally epic in style, the spirit and sometimes the details of lyric: there are debts to Pindar and Alcaeus. More, he has the capacity to hold together without incongruity a variety of audiences: religious devotees at a festival, the imperial Court (the themes of politics and patronage are both there), and his literary and scholarly contemporaries. It is this extraordinary flexibility and variety which gives the *Hymns* their continuing power to fascinate even when (as for us) the basis of the particular religious beliefs has disintegrated. But the variety is a variety in unity. The unity for each hymn is provided by the deity addressed, linked to a particular myth and presented in the context of a particular occasion. The unity for the whole collection is provided by Callimachus's unique mind. For these factors which we analyze are not separate units to be glued together in an uneasy whole, but the natural expression of a single self-disciplined, carefully integrated person.

CHAPTER 8

The Epigrams

I   The Epigram before Callimachus

AN epigram means something that is inscribed. The earliest of all verse epigrams is inscribed on an Attic Dipylon vase. The majority were inscribed on stone. They naturally tend to be short, often only two lines in length, and this of itself leads to an economical and pointed style. They are in a variety of meters, though the hexameter and the elegiac couplet predominate. They are naturally principally used for epitaphs and votive offerings. An epigram today tends to mean a witticism, a dwarfish, waspish whole with a sting in the tail. Although some early epigrams have point, their use was such that wit would have been totally inappropriate. It was only later, when the epigram became an artificial literary form that wit became remotely appropriate, and it was only with the overpowering miniature genius of the Roman Martial that this meaning tended to predominate: even in Martial there are plenty of epigrams of beauty and tenderness: witness the exquisite lines on the dead child Erotion (5, 34 cf 37). The elegiac couplet came to be the chief, though never the sole medium for the epigram. It will be noticed that there is no absolute distinction between an elegy (in the ancient sense) and an epigram (in the ancient sense). This can be interestingly seen later in the arrangement of the poems of Catullus. They were probably published in three scrolls. Numbers 1-60 consist of shortish poems in a variety of meters, and would have formed one scroll. Numbers 61-64 are longer poems totalling some 800 lines. Numbers 65-68 are certainly elegies and total a little over 300 lines. Numbers 69-116 are shorter elegiac poems, and are often called epigrams. It is not quite certain whether 65-68 were "bound in with" the longer

poems or the epigrams. Further, the powerful 76th poem is 26
lines long, and it is hard not to call it an elegy; equally it is hard to
dissociate it from some of the more epigrammatic treatments of
ambiguous love. Elegy is extended epigram; epigram is contracted elegy.

Simonides was the first discernible genius in the development
of the literary epigram. Unfortunately, his reputation was such
that all manner of epigrams were attributed to him, and we
cannot be certain which are his. Even the authorship of the
famous epigram of the dead at Thermopylae—

> Passer-by, tell them in Sparta that we lie here
> in obedience to their words. (Hdt. 7, 228)

has been questioned. What is certain is that he gave the form
literary impetus, and throughout the fifth century epigram
flourished. The Persian Wars helped to concentrate on the
celebration of patriotic death. Aeschylus, Sophocles, and Euripides all used the medium, and Euripides was so commemorated
by Ion of Samos. Large numbers of elegant, strong, anonymous
verses have survived on stone.[1] So far as we can see the practice
continued unabated through the fourth century. Plato was
perhaps the greatest artist of the epigram, but it was an art
widely cultivated. Another fine epigrammatist from the fourth
century was Erinna from the small island of Telos: she pointed
the way for other women writers, Anyte and Nossis. In the fourth
century too epigram was used in literary controversy, notably by
Theocritus of Chios.

With the Hellenistic Age the epigram came into its own.
Asclepiades, one of Callimachus's Telchines, was writing before
him. He was an exponent of love, often moving towards the
obscene. Phalaecus, who had the eleven-syllable line named
Phalaecean after him, was an inventive but minor writer.
Callimachus's older contemporary, Theocritus, wrote epigrams
using a variety of meters; these included dedicatory inscriptions
and epitaphs; some dealt with love, others with personal themes;
one group took famous poets as its theme. The one really
important figure in this connection was Leonidas of Tarentum, a
minor writer but an interesting one. He was, or pretended to be,
a realist and wrote about the hardships of working-class life, of

fishermen and other peasants. He was certainly a pessimist. His
themes stand in curious contrast with his style which is
extravagant and almost baroque. In this he is poles apart from
Callimachus. Leonidas had his admirers, and his verses were
imitated for centuries. But none of the others has the range or
control of Callimachus. Callimachus was the real creator of the
Hellenistic epigram.

II *Callimachus: Themes and Moods*

Callimachus's epigrams have for the most part survived
through the Palatine Anthology, a collection from the Byzantine
period covering many moods and many centuries. A few survive
through quotation by other writers, two by the gossiping
biographer of philosophers, Diogenes Laertius, two by Sextus
Empiricus, again for their philosophical interest, one by the
geographer Strabo, one (because of its relevance) by the author
of *The Life of Aratus,* one only (surprisingly, since Callimachus's
lore was curious and precise) by Athenaeus in *The Professors at
Dinner,* two by the ancient annotator of Dionysius of Thrace, one
in an anonymous miscellany from Paris. Only two of these do not
also appear in the Anthology. But there are also quotations of
phrases from epigrams which do not appear in the Anthology,
cited by Diogenes Laertius in his life of Euclid of Megara, or by
Athenaeus or by Stephanus of Byzantium or by the Aristotelian
commentator Eustratius, or by writers on metrics, or by
anonymous biographers or scholiasts. This makes it fairly certain
that the anthologists were—ultimately, since the Anthology
grew out of earlier anthologies—using selectively a collection of
the poet's epigrams. We cannot be certain that these formed a
section of his corpus of works as he planned to publish them, or
whether he regarded them as trivia and some pious disciple
brought them together: if the latter, there is a certain irony, for if
he is remembered at all widely today outside the world of
scholarship it is for "Heraclitus" (2). The majority of university
students of the classics, if they have read him at all, will have
read that and a few more epigrams in *The Oxford Book of Greek
Verse* or elsewhere. A couple of epigrams, otherwise attributed
in the Anthology, are given to Callimachus by other authors: we
should assume that their memory was at fault.

Callimachus was the Housman of antiquity. He had formidable learning, combative pugnacity, and a rare capacity to put both aside and write with exquisite simplicity. In the epigrams the learning does not obtrude. Of course it is there: once a polymath always a polymath. A. E. Housman could not and did not wish to avoid echoes of Shakespeare, or classical references, even in phrasing like the Latin "sum of things." Callimachus will tell an anecdote of Pittacus (1), claim with references *The Capture of Oechalia* for Creophylus rather than Homer (6), see Aratus's poetry in the line of descent from Hesiod's, following its purple passages and omitting the gray (27), toss off Homeric references (e.g., 48, 2; 61, 3), write a verse based on Stoic logic and ethics (42), or call water "Achelous" (29). But most of these are slight; they represent, so to say, the man behind the epigram rather than the epigram itself, which relies on other qualities for its point.

The combative spirit of *Ibis* and *Iambi* peers through some epigrams too.

> I hate epic poetry. I have no liking for a road
>   carrying crowds all over the place.
> I detest a roaming lover. I do not drink from an open well.
>   I abominate all that's popular.
> Lysanies, oh yes, you're handsome, handsome. But before I say
>   it clearly,
>   Echo answers "And someone else's."   (28)

Here Callimachus brings together his rejection of the epic, popular and hackneyed, with his rejection of a boy who spreads his favors. The repeated "I hate," "I have no liking," "I detest," "I abominate," show an intensity of emotion which starts from a literary judgment: "abominate" *(sikchaino)* is actually imported from prose for the climax. This is countered by the cry *kalos kalos,* a love word. But Echo shows the poet to be self-deceived: *naichi kalos* is echoed by *kallos echei,* "and another possesses him": Lysanies too is a roamer.[2] A fragment attacks Antimachus of Colophon's *Lyde* (entitled from his girl friend) as "too fat and shapeless a writing" (398). In general, however, Callimachus, like Housman, kept his pugnacity in check in his epigrams. Occasionally he dons a persona to let it break through. Timon was a famous misanthrope.

> "Timon, now you are dead, which do you loathe, darkness or
>   light."
>   "Darkness. More of you in Hades." (4)

Callimachus is characteristically playing with a common euphemism by which the dead were called "the majority". As to the pugnacity, he liked playing with names; his means "Glory in battle".

But without necessarily attacking others he makes his literary values clear even here. "Theaetetus took an untrodden track": he deserves first prize: even if he does not get it, he will be remembered when the prize-winners are forgotten (7). A rather heavily witty epigram suggests that when a poet wins, his response is brief: "Victory!" When he loses he goes off into long rigmaroles. There is some underlying implication that brevity represents inspiration, long-windedness the lack of it (8). The epigram on Aratus (27) is a further assertion of Callimachus's advocacy of Hesiod as a model. More, he applauds *Phaenomena* and calls it "Aratus's energetic sleeplessness". Here too is a judgment. Fine writing means hard work and burning the midnight oil: Horace in *Ars Poetica* was to say much the same thing. There is some reference to Theocritus, of whom Callimachus approved. One epigram compares Theocritus to Ganymede, perhaps implicitly Ptolemy to Zeus. There is warm personal affection and a closely allusive knowledge of Theocritus's poems (52). Another is a curious fragment of literary history:

> Astacides, the goatherd from Crete, was stolen away from
>   the hill by a Nymph.
>   Astacides is now holy.
> No more shall we shepherds sing of Daphnis under the oaks of
> Dicte, only of Astacides. (22)

The threefold repetition of the name makes it fairly certain that this is humorous. Astacides is perhaps Leonidas of Tarentum, the epigrammatist: Astacus = Leon = lobster; he also appears as Lycidas of Crete in Theocritus's seventh idyll. This is no epitaph: more likely Leonidas has gone off with a girl. The poem itself is an affectionate parody of the artifices of pastoral poets.

Callimachus, like Webster, was much possessed by death. So,

to continue the parallel, was Housman: the last line of *A Shropshire Lad* is "When I am dead and gone," of *Last Poems* "And to earth I." There is more to this for Callimachus than the fact that, at least since Simonides, the epitaph was one of the more obvious and popular forms of epigram—and a particularly obvious one to anthologize. Callimachus wrote an epitaph for his father:

> You who are walking past my tomb, know that I am son and father
>   of Callimachus of Cyrene.
> You should know both. One commanded his country's armies:
>   the other wrote poems beyond envy's reach.
> Small wonder! When the Muses look on people favorably in youth,
>   they remain friends with their gray hairs.
>   (21)

One recalls the remark of Abraham Mendelssohn, son of the philosopher and father of the composer: "I used to be the son of my father, but now I am the father of my son." Callimachus also wrote a mock-epitaph for himself:

> You're passing the tomb of Battus's son, a man who understood
>   poetry—
>   and the time to laugh and drink. (35)

The laughter here has to do with the gift of producing lighter verse.

No clearly consistent picture of death emerges from Callimachus. The most he can say is that death is a sacred sleep, as in the epitaph on Saon (9). This is repeated in one of his most charming poems:

> Crethis with her many tales, skilled in lightness and loveliness,
>   is often missed by the Samians' daughters,
> their delightful fellow-worker, never stopping talking. Here
>   she is sleeping
>   the sleep that comes to all girls. (16)

The sleep of death is a recurring theme in Housman too. The word "Here" is important; in Greek it means "in this world," "here on earth." Callimachus has no belief in the lore of the Underworld. In the epitaph on Timarchus he writes of the Abode of the Righteous (10), but this is hardly more than a conventional though sincere compliment to a good man. The Timon epigram too paints the traditional picture, but for the sake of epigrammatic point. More telling is "Charidas":

> "Is Charidas at rest underneath?" "If you mean Arimmas's son
>   from Cyrene, he is underneath."
> "Charidas, what of the underworld?" "Deep darkness." "The road
>   up?" "A lie."
>   "Pluto?" "A myth." "Ruined!"
> "These words you've heard are not absurd. But if you want
>   cheerful news,
>   a large ox is dirt-cheap in Hades." (13)

The last line has punning point: literally, "a large ox is valued at an ox from Pella," that is a Macedonian coin of small value, with an ox stamped on it. The purport is clear. Death is no respecter of earthly values, and no respecter of persons. The myths are false, there is no hope.

To Callimachus, as to Housman, love is in general blighted. But homosexuality is in Callimachus uninhibited, whereas in Housman its repression became a strongly creative force in his writing. With Callimachus the stream runs shallower. Still, pessimism is there. The episodes of Erigone or Psamathe or Cydippe in *Aitia*, or the story of Galatea, do not exactly show the course of true love running smooth, and if in the epigrams Callimachus represents a conventional or artificial situation, it is significant that his conventional or artificial situations are tinged with gloom. An inherent pessimism was here reinforced by the tendencies of the age. The breakup of the city-state before world empires and of the family before increased mobility led to a greater individual freedom. This led to an interest in the psychology of falling in love, which can be seen in Apollonius, and the psychology of passion generally, with an inevitable interest in abnormal and frustrated passion, alike because they were more interesting and because they mirrored some of the social frustrations of the time. So in Callimachus we have a *paraclausithyron*, that is, a serenade before a closed door, with a curse for the callous girl within (63), and another poem, which we might call a *metaparaclausithyron*, in which the poet apologizes for a serenade which evidently left the door resolutely shut (42). Love is a consuming fire which wastes its victims (43; 44); it is a disease which needs remedies (46); it is a predatory hunt (31). Here is an example which attracted the attention of the early Roman poet Q. Lutatius: there are some textual uncertainties.

Half of my soul is still breathing, half either Love or Death
  has grabbed: I can't see which.
Has she gone back to one of the boys? I warned them off time
                                  and again:
  "She's a runaway, kids, don't touch her."
Join me in the chase there. That's where, fit for hanging, crossed in
  love, somewhere she's flitting. (41)

So too, in a poem that influenced Catullus, we find Callignotus abandoning Ionis for a boy (25), and in another of which Horace showed awareness, Cleonicus, poor fellow, mere skin and bones for love (30).

Callimachus's remedy was Housman's, though his tipple was wine rather than ale, and the great nineteenth-century German student of the epigram, R. Reitzenstein, rightly identified the class of sympotic epigrams. This may be readily illustrated:

Top up. Repeat the shout "To Diocles!" Achelous does not
                                  recognize
  the ladles consecrated to Diocles.
He's a handsome lad, Achelous, not half he isn't. If anyone
                                  says No,
  may my knowledge of beauty be confined to the study! (29)

The epigram is obscure. The river god Achelous stands for water, and the point is a toast in neat wine to the object of love. The ending is slightly odd: the sense must be that, even if others deny it, Diocles is handsome, and the poet will wager that at forfeit of practical experience. Others of the love poems are clearly sympotic in origin. But even drink does not give security, for through it Menecrates came to his fated sleep (61). Housman, like Horace, can use drink as an escape from the thought of death. Even that is denied Callimachus.

But Callimachus had religious beliefs which Housman lacked.

They can be seen especially in the group of dedicatory epigrams. At their best they show a simple and touching faith, as in

> Artemis, here's a statue offered you by Phileratis.
> Accept it, Lady; preserve her. (33)

or

> Once again, Lady Eilithyia, come at Lycaenis's call,
>   and bless her bearing,
> that your shrine may have another gift of incense,
>   now for a girl, next for a boy. (53).

Even if the faith belongs primarily to the offerer of the dedication, it is hard not to think that Callimachus shared it.

Callimachus was interested in current philosophical trends. One epigram, his excuse for an offensive serenade, uses the Stoic distinction between motive and act (42). Another honors a contemporary philosopher named Timarchus (10). Another relates the famous story of Cleombrotus committing suicide after reading Plato's *Phaedo* (23). The philosophers moralized about the iniquity of seafaring, and Callimachus, like other poets, takes up the theme from them (17; 18). The longest of the epigrams is a piece of moralizing, the story of a man with two possible brides, one upper-class and wealthy, asking the advice of Pittacus, who tells him to listen to boys playing with tops. "Keep your own place" they say to one another (1).

III   *Callimachus: Imagery and Technique*

The primary impression left by the epigrams is of simplicity: it seems effortless but it is firmly controlled by craftmanship. Some examples from the epitaphs will serve.

> His father Philippus laid to rest his twelve-year-old son
>   here, his high hope, Nicoteles. (19)

Every word is significant; there is nothing forced or extraneous; it is perfection in miniature, like a Hilliard painting or a verse by

Housman. Its one obvious artifice lies in alliteration, again a device of Housman, in the original a meticulously organized pattern of *p* against *d* and *t*. Another couplet closely similar in this apparent simplicity is the epitaph for Saon:

> Here Saon, Dion's son, from Acanthus in sacred rest sleeps:
>   death is not for the righteous. (9)

Here again simplicity is exquisite. There is slight alliteration, *k* cutting through and then softening away. The epigram is pointed by the juxtaposition of sleep and death, and the chiastic structure. But the image is of the simplest and basically here too not a word is wasted or over-elaborate.

A third example is the most famous of the epigrams.

> Heraclitus, someone told me of your death and brought me to
>   a tear.
>   I remembered how often we two
> saw the sun down in talk. Somewhere, I suppose, friend from
>   Halicarnassus,
>   you are long long long long ago dust.
> But your nightingales live on; on them that comprehensive
>   burglar,
>   Death, shall not lay hand. (2)

Here the artifices are more obvious; the imagery richer; the fourth line, shaped in Greek

> friend Halicarnassian fourpastly dust

so that two simple nouns frame two long qualifiers, one seemingly the poet's invention; in the original two balancing examples, in the first and last lines, of the device called tmesis, the division of a single word or phrase into two; the helpless ambiguity of "somewhere."

Another example is in iambics, accompanying a dedication; ancient authorities suggested the verse should be presented in three long lines, but the first line is cited as an integral unit, and Wilamowitz may be right in supposing that the epigram was designed to be inscribed on a quiver:

> Menitas of Lyctus
> offered the bow with these
> words "Here, Sarapis,
> I'm giving you a longbow
> and quiver; the arrows
> are with the men of Hesperis." (37)

The only word that is remotely strained is "longbow," literally "horn," originally one of the two horn-tips of the Scythian rather than the Cretan bow, but it does not obtrude.

Callimachus achieves this simplicity with the most unpromising material. Here is a dedicatory couplet for a statue.

> For Inachus's Isis Thales's daughter Aeschylis stands.
> Eirene, her mother, promised. (57)

It is no ordinary skill which has woven a pattern to all intents and purposes out of five proper names and four other simple words.

Another example, a dedication to Heracles, is particularly illuminating:

> O Lord, Lion-Strangler, Boar-Killer, I'm an oak-bough
>   dedicated to you.
>   "By whom?" Archinus. "Which?" The Cretan. "Accepted."
>   (34)

Here the point lies in the contrast between the elaborately coined language of the first line and the laconic treatment of the second; the god seems to be cutting off what he fears may be an inflated eulogy.

One example of Callimachus's economy is to be seen in his use of descriptive adjectives. The advice to the prospective writer "Always blot your finest passages" is never more applicable than to adjectives. There are whole verses of English hymns which can be shortened by a foot without altering the sense and with advantage to the strength, by cutting out an epithet from each line. Callimachus is too burnished a writer to fall into the snare of that kind of writing. In the epitaph on Heraclitus there is no adjective at all, save "Halicarnassian." In general, descriptive adjectives are rare in Callimachus, and never otiose. Sometimes they are words of simple description which the ear scarcely notices as separate and blends with the noun: "his high hope"

(19), "simple life" (26), "Dear Earth" (26), "good nurse" (50).
Sometimes they are precise and factual, "twelve-year-old" (19),
"Phrygian" (50). Occasionally, but only occasionally, they are
used as powerful instruments of emotion:

> Lycus of Naxos did not die on land; at sea he watched
>   ship and life destroyed together,
> when sailing from Aegina on trade. He is a corpse in the
>   water,
>   I a tomb uselessly bearing his name,
> announcing this true word: "Avoid tangling with the sea,
>   sailor, when the Kids are setting." (18)

"True" or rather "utterly true" gains strength by its very
isolation.

One of the most eloquent features of Callimachus's epigrams is
the fascination that proper names held for him. We may compare
an epitaph in St. Olave's, Southwark, on Mr. Munday, dating from
the sixteenth century:

> Hallowed be the Sabbath
> And farewell all worldly Pelfe;
> The weeke begins on Tuesday,
> For Munday hath hang'd himself.

The presence of a pun, it will be noted, does not make the name
fictitious. The name Aceson which appears with point in one
epigram (54) happens to be recorded from Cyrene. Even in the
seemingly simplest epitaphs of Callimachus there may be a
further level of meaning. Thus "Saon, Dicon's son, from
Acanthus" means something like "Justus Wright of Thornbury,"
and this is the poem's point (9).

The Nicoteles epitaph is another example. The simplicity is
real, but is also deceptive. The verse is shaped to end on the
pathetic irony of the boy's name—Victor. More, the father's
name, Philippus, means "lover of horses." Recognizing this, we
can see that "his high hope" means in racing parlance "the
favorite" and "laid to rest" means "sent to the knackers." The
result, except that names mean less to us, is more like:

> Mr Ryder Senior retired his twelve-year old son
>   here, the favorite, Victor. (19)

The epitaph on Lycus (18) contains the same point with brilliant irony; the last line is a warning to sailors to avoid the sea when the Kids are setting, a group of stars in Auriga often associated with bad weather. Lycus means Wolf. It is usually the Wolf who devours the Kids; here the Kids have devoured the Wolf. There are other slighter examples. Aeschra ("Ugly") was a good milk, that is a good nurse, and the name and epithet are put alongside one another in a startling oxymoron; and Miccus ("Tiny") was not small in generosity (50); here the play depends on paradox. Aceson ("Doc") pays a debt to Asclepius, god of healing (54). Micylus ("Tich") had little resources, and asks the earth to be light upon him (26). Conopion ("Gnat") gives her lover sleepless nights (63). One quotation on a victorious gamecock includes not only the owner's name, Euaenetus ("Glorious"), but his father's name Phaedrus ("Brilliant") and his grandfather's Philoxenus ("Hospitable"). There may be some family reason for including the grandfather, or there may be a punning allusion which we have lost.

The same punning mood is displayed over ordinary words in one epigram. Its meaning lies on the surface, and the greatest of all English classical scholars, Richard Bentley, who exercised his ingenuity on it, did so to excess:

> This comes from the salt—on his board Eudemus ate cheap salt.
>   The strong storms—of debt—passed him by.
> He offered it to the gods of Samothrace saying "Friends, my
>   vow is fulfilled.
>   From salt I found salvation and make offering." (47)

It is difficult to translate. Dedications, often of a model ship, were common from shipwrecked sailors, and there is an example to the Cabeiri, who were identified with the gods of Samothrace, in Cairo Museum. When we hear "This comes from the salt" we think of such a dedication; "on (his) board" carries on the illusion; then we realize that it is a saltcellar. Callimachus, rightly, does not let go of the joke, and continues it through the storms of debt, and in the last line where "From salt" is ambiguous between "Saved from the sea" and "Saved through salt." It is slight, amiable, ingenious.

Another technique of wit—it is actually taken from rhetoric— is exaggeration or overstatement. Martial used it brilliantly, as

with the thin man trying to blow a trumpet and falling through it,
or the short man dropping something and needing a ladder to get
it. Here is a subtle example from Callimachus.

Cheer up, you on Cynthus, Echemmas of Crete has offered his bow
    to Artemis in Ortygia,
the bow which cleared the mountain-range of you. But he's stopped
                                     now, goats;
    the goddess has negotiated a truce. (62)

Cynthus is a small hill, not a mountain-range; it is on Delos, and
there were never any wild goats there; and if there had been, it
is sacred, and hunting would not have been allowed. The whole
is a whimsical blow-up of an archer's skill, enhanced by the
thought that "Cretans are always liars"; the epigram, though in
the third person, is written as if spoken by Echemmas.

   Series iuncturaque pollet, declared Horace, "it is the placing
and juxtaposition of words which is effective," and was himself
the master of such effects.[3] So, in his own way, was Callimachus.
The first half of his pentameters repays scrutiny. Sometimes he
uses it to juxtapose two names, and add to the effect of each. His
most powerful effects arise from the juxtaposition of two verbs.
Four particularly startling examples spring to mind. In "The Epic
and the Lover" (28) after his crescendo "I hate," "I have no
liking," "I detest," he puts in "I do not drink" before "I
abominate." The effect is to bring together "drink: abominate."
He has not drunk but it is as if he drinks and spits it out. A second
example comes from "Diocles" (29) where the final line begins
"says, know." Others may *say* No, he *knows,* but the conjunction
of statement and prayer ("May I know") produces a kind of
cross-rhythm. A third is in "Heraclitus" (2) "brought, remembered"; with the tear the indefinite messenger is replaced by a
definite "I," the external news by an internal response; but it is
subtle, for the tear calls up the memory, not the memory the
tear, and this leads us forward to the plaintive "nightingales." A
fourth from "Saon" (9) where the juxtaposition of sleep and
death is exquisite and poignant. Each of these effects is in its way
original.
   A similar though slighter example of effect depending on
position is to be seen in Callimachus's coining of new or
employment of rare words. In no fewer than three poems he uses

a word not found elsewhere as his point, the final, the climactic
moment. One is the superlative which ends a bitter little verse.

> I know my hands are empty of money, but, by the Graces,
>   Menippus,
>   don't "tell me of my own dream."

i.e., rub it in, tell me what I know already—

> It's grim enough to hear it—pierces me through and through.
> Yes, dear, of all you ever did the unloverliest. (32)

Again, in a poignant epitaph on a dead sailor buried by a living
sailor, the climactic word is otherwise unattested:

> Who are you, stranger from some shipwreck? Leontichus found
>   your body
>   here on the beach, and laid you in this tomb
> with tears for the dangers of his own profession. He has
>   no life of quiet,
>   but like a gull sea-ranges. (58)

This is peculiarly effective. We do not need to look beyond the
literal meaning: yet the image of "a sea of troubles" is at least as
old as Aeschylus, and Callimachus surely intends his poem as a
commentary on the life of man. A third example shows a more
flippant mood. When a poet wins, his response is brief—
"Victory!" So the poet ends his six lines "Let mine, Lord, be
brachysyllabic."

An elaborate treatment of meter would be out of place.
Callimachus's hexameters move swiftly, and he effects this by
avoiding a strong caesura in the third foot; often there is a
marked break after a weak caesura at that point. In the longest of
the epigrams, the anecdote about Pittacus (1), all the hexameters
have the weak caesura. The pace is further established by the
frequency of dactyls. Bucolic diaeresis, an emphatic break
coinciding with the end of the fourth foot, is common: sometimes
it helps to drive the hexameter on to the pentameter. In one
unique instance there is elision between hexameter and pentameter, creating a single unit (41, 1). The pentameter usually
has a clear break at the halfway point, but occasionally
Callimachus keeps the line moving by an elision over the

caesura. Usually Callimachus uses the couplet as his unit of thought. The hexameter swings on to the following line, where the first half of the pentameter checks it and lets it run down to the end of the couplet. The couplet is most frequently self-contained. Sometimes, however, he uses a kind of counterrhythm by carrying the sense from one couplet to the next. Three poems, one much mangled in our manuscripts, are in various forms of iambic (37-9), and the fragments include a hendecasyllabic line (395), the only surviving trochaic pentameters from ancient literature, a meter apparently particularly identified with Callimachus (399), some Asclepiads (400), and some Pherecrateans (401). The variety is impressive; the remains too fragmentary to allow an evaluation of the poet's metrical skill and versatility.

Neither alliteration nor assonance is overdone. There are some controlled alliterative effects, as in "Nicoteles" (19). The most extraordinary assonance comes in "Charidas" (13), here translated "The words you've heard are not absurd": this is the dead man's impatient insistence on what he's saying. Rhyme between the two parts of the pentameter is a likely concomitant of an inflected language. Its comparative infrequency suggests that Callimachus deliberately avoided it except for special effects. He uses it in the last line of the epitaphs on Nicoteles (19) and Lycus (18); in the former it is ingenious as the rhyming words do not in fact agree grammatically; in the latter it rounds off the sad words with peculiar power; in both it adds a certain finality. There is one double epitaph, for a brother and sister who died on the same day (20); the effect occurs twice, expressing the "double . . . trouble," words which indeed form one of the rhyming pairs.

Imagery is seldom elaborate, but effectively used. A good example is in a poem of escape from love:

> There's something—yes by Pan!—hidden, there's something
> here
>   by Dionysus!—a fire beneath the ashes.
> I've no confidence, so don't entangle me: often, unseen,
>   a tranquil river gnaws at a wall.
> And now I'm terrified, Menexenus, that, slipping in,
> this Alsatian
>   may throw me into Love's grasp. (44)

"Alsatian" renders *sigerpes*, a proposal of Bentley's, a hound which cannot be trusted. Here we have three principal images: the fire beneath the ashes, the river eating at the wall, the treacherous hound. But others come in, "entangle," "gnawing," "slipping in," "throw," although they are unobtrusive. Another poem of similar length and similar theme is similar in structure:

> The visitor had an unseen wound. How painful a sigh
>   he raised from the heart (did you notice?)
> as he drank his third cup, and the roses from the fellow's
>   garlands shed
>   their petals and lay on the ground.
> He's badly roasted all right. Good God! my guess isn't off
>   the beat.
>   Set a thief to catch a thief. (43)

Here the central couplet is purely descriptive, though the rose shedding its petals is a vivid symbol of the wastage of love. Before it we have the wound of love, an image used also by Theocritus. The third couplet contains three images. The first portrays love as a fire, as in the previous poem, and often elsewhere, but here the effect is more grotesque, though paralleled in Sophocles and Theocritus. The second, a difficult phrase not precisely paralleled, seems to be from dancing. The third, the reason for his capacity to see through the stranger, comes from crime; it does not appear to be proverbial in Greek as in English. The fire of love recurs; in the poem to Cleonicus (30), there is a side-glance at it, where the lover is reduced to skin and bones, and the poet invokes the piercing sun with this love-shrivelled specimen before him. These are variations on a theme; Callimachus can hardly avoid the theme, however hackneyed, but he plays on it pleasantly. Love as a sickness or disease is the theme of another rather charming verse (46).

Another of the images of love is that of the hunt or chase. This is successfully developed in one epigram which Horace valued enough to take up.[4]

> Epicydes, the mountain-hunter, trails every hare,
>   and the roe-deer's spoor
> through snow and ice. Yet if anyone says "Look! here's
>   an animal
>   already shot!" he won't touch it.

> My love's like that. It's happy chasing the hard-to-get;
>   it ignores easy prey. (31)

This is an excellent conceit; the same thought is handled more clumsily or in a more conventional manner elsewhere (41; 45).

A few more images deserve notice: the storms of debt (47); the sailor, restless as a gull (58); the crumb of fear (46); the nurse described as "milk" (50); death the burglar (2). Some of them refer to poetry: verses sweet as honey (a deliberate cliché) (27); the poet of originality refusing to drink from the common well (28). The most successful of these is the description of Heraclitus's poems as "nightingales" (2). The suggestion that this was the title of his collected poems, and should be printed with a capital, however tempting, is needless. It is an excellent image, alike in the liquid music it attributes to the author, the plaintive quality, the survival beyond human life represented in the various myths of the nightingale.

Callimachus uses imagery, but limits its use. Five of the sixty-odd poems depend on it; not more than another five contain significant images. Except the last (and that is uncertain) none of the images is original, but the treatment is careful and controlled; we expect Alexandria to produce a rational treatment of traditional material rather than a fresh creativity.

IV   *Conclusion*

When Martial, unchallenged premier among Roman epigrammatists, wanted to compliment his contemporary Brutianus's essays in the Greek epigram he represented him as receiving the palm from Callimachus.[5] Flattery apart, to Martial Callimachus among the Greeks was *the* epigrammatist. It is not a judgment which would be easy to dispute.

CHAPTER 9

Prose Works

I *Introduction*

CALLIMACHUS evidently had to his name a substantial nonpoetic output, as we have already noticed, and we will look briefly at individual items. To all intents and purposes nothing is left except for a collection of excerpts from his *Encyclopaedia of Worldwide Marvels arranged Geographically*, put together by Antigonus of Carystus. These excerpts make it clear that Callimachus's volumes were themselves little more than an anthology of extracts from earlier historians, geographers, and scientific philosophers—Aristotle, Ctesias, Eudoxus, Heraclides, Lyco, Megasthenes, Nicagoras, Phanias, Polycritus, Theophrastus, Theopompus, Xenophilus. We may be impressed by the range of Callimachus's interests and reading, by his capacity to excerpt succinctly and relevantly, by his powers of organization and analysis. It does not add anything to our appreciation of him as a writer, except perhaps to note with interest that a man who was so concerned with style could be so self-effacing. It seems likely that the large majority of prose titles attributed to him fall into this general category: they represent catalogues, lists, classifications, anthologies, collections. The one exception, *Against Praxiphanes*, is the one prose work whose absence the majority of us seriously regret. The rest will have contained much useful and fascinating information, but they can hardly be called works of literature.

II *The* Catalogue

Undoubtedly the most formidable of Callimachus's scholarly undertakings was the organization of the Library and production of the *Catalogue*, known in antiquity as the *Pinaces* or *Tablets*. In

154

full it was the *Catalogue of writers eminent in all literature and
of their works.* It was a monumental work. Zenodotus and his
other assistants had done some preliminary spadework on the
arrangement, Zenodotus organizing epic and lyric, Alexander of
Pleuron tragedy and Lycophron of Chalcis comedy, but the rest
of the arrangement and all the cataloguing were Callimachus's
achievement.

Callimachus began by a broad classification of the library
under literary genres, epic, lyric, drama, oratory, history, law,
rhetorical theory, and miscellaneous. Some authors would fit
neatly and completely under one of these headings: others,
whose output was itself more miscellaneous, would have their
work divided. Within each class the authors were put in
alphabetical order, and Callimachus appended a brief biographical notice of each, which must have involved quite a lot of
detailed research. Each author's works under each heading were
classified in alphabetical order. Again this entailed research into
evidence of authenticity. Titles were often uncertain or ambiguous, so for clarification Callimachus appended the opening
words. As a bibliographical detail he also recorded the number
of lines. A typical entry is recorded by Athenaeus (6, 244A):
"Writers on Meals: Chaerephon *On the Pod:* 'Since you have
often commanded me': 375 lines."

The whole catalogue amounted to 120 volumes. The title *The
Museum* which is recorded among his works perhaps refers to
this whole work. *Catalogue and Chronological List of Dramatic
Poets from the beginning of Drama* presumably constituted one
or more volumes of the whole, but we notice that it had an
additional elaboration in the form of the chronological treatment. Another subsection which ran to several volumes is also
recorded by Athenaeus (13, 585B) under the general heading
Customs; we can again reconstruct the entry: "Gnathaena
Dinner-table Customs: 'The following custom is egalitarian and
democratic': 323 lines." This either fell under the legislative or
the miscellaneous section. *The Dictionary (Pinax) of the
Language and Compositions of Democritus* may have been a
subsection of the full *Catalogue* or a by-product of it; it sounds as
if it may have included some analysis of Democritus's linguistic
usages.

Such an enormous undertaking could hardly be faultless. A
papyrus fragment of a commentary on Bacchylides shows that

Aristarchus criticized Callimachus for including *Cassandra*
among the paeans, whereas it was really a dithyramb.[1] One
recalls the story of Dr. Johnson's rejoinder to the woman who
asked why in his *Dictionary* he did not conform to the normal
usage of "fetlock," expecting a learned justification: "Ignorance,
madam, sheer ignorance." Perhaps Callimachus would not have
been so candid. Aristophanes of Byzantium later produced a
major work *On Callimachus's Catalogue* which consisted of
errata and *addenda*. Athenaeus shows that Aristophanes was
interested in precise usage, as in the distinction between "over
the hand" (a ritual wash before a meal) and "washing up"
(cleaning your fingers of stickiness after a meal). But Callimachus's classification of the library lasted, and his published
Catalogue was the basis of all such future work.

III   Other Prose Works

For the rest we have little more than titles. Many of them are
lexical. The Peripatetic practice of collecting, recording, and
analyzing information was at the basis of the Museum, and
Callimachus came under the spell of its methodology. We have
the impression of a systematic, wide-ranging mind, not afraid to
be categorized as "miscellaneous," a snapper-up of unconsidered
trifles from all quarters, a practitioner of serendipity who
organized his casual findings into a body of knowledge. It is
reminiscent of the late Reginald Reynolds who wrote two
fascinating books of curious learning on *Beds* and *Beards*. *The
Customs of Foreigners* shows ethnographical interests of the
type evinced by Hecataeus, Herodotus, and Hellanicus in
previous generations. It may be an offshoot of his classificatory
work on *Customs*.

Local nomenclature comprises material he may have been
collecting at the same time: it analyzed different accounts of the
same object in different areas. This, it seems, was a large work
with a number of separate sections. It is almost certain that
Different Names of Fishes was one of these sections, highly
probable that *Local Names of Months* was another, not
implausible that *Foundations and Changes of Name of Islands
and Cities* was a third, and at least possible that *Winds* and *Birds*
belonged to the same work. Certainly in the apparently scientific
titles there is a probability that his interest lay in language rather

than physical or biological research. He seems, however, to have
had some interest in geography. We can trace this in his interest
in local lore: he goes to some trouble in his poetry to get this
right. A particular interest was in rivers. One title is *The Rivers of
the World,* with what are presumably the titles of subsections,
The Rivers of Europe and *The Rivers of Asia.* It is significant too
that some of his more miscellaneous collections of information
were classified geographically: *Encyclopaedia of Worldwide
Marvels arranged Geographically.* Here again we should assume
that *Unusual Marvels of the Peloponnese and Italy* was one
volume of the wider work. Clearly a geographical classification
was one convenient way of organizing the material for ready
reference: we see the mind of the cataloguer at work. Such a
collection will have contained a good deal of mythological and
aetiological material: one suspects that it was an important
source-book for *Aitia,* though he had of course to glean the
material from elsewhere first. *Historical Notes* may also have
been a source-book of aetiological material. We would have
expected more titles referring to mythology, but there is one
only, and that not certainly, *On the Nymphs.*

One work stands apart from these. This is *Against Praxiphanes.*
We know something of Praxiphanes. He was an Aristotelian
philosopher with whom Aratus and Callimachus had at one time
studied, and however much Callimachus may later have become
disaffected from him, it was no doubt from him that he learned
about the scientific methodology of research whether in
scientific subjects or in the humanities—the patient, thorough
collection of material with careful and accurate observation and
recording, the organization of that material in accessible and
usable ways, and the drawing of generalized conclusions. But
Praxiphanes appears as one of the Telchines, according to the
scholiast, one of Callimachus's opponents in poetic theory, and
his association with Rhodes makes this likely. Praxiphanes wrote
books on *Poets* and *Poetry.* The approach will have been
Aristotelian and traditional, based on the systematic examination
of what had been successfully done in the past, and *ipso facto*
hostile to innovation of the kind which Callimachus practiced.
Brink has argued that he would believe in the long poem with
organic unity.[2] We may reasonably suppose that Callimachus's
reply was in part rhetorical invective, a counterattack on
Praxiphanes and his views, but in part a prose defense of his own

practice, the loss of which we must deplore. Pfeiffer has rightly warned us against overstating Callimachus's opposition to Aristotelian principles, but certainly the discontinuous form of *Aitia* was something new and different. As Praxiphanes was born about 340, this work by Callimachus can hardly be later than about 270.

One other work must be mentioned. This in the Greek is called *Peri logadon*, and the title is mysterious. It might be taken to mean *On picked soldiers* or *On picked stones* or, just possibly, *On men of eloquence*. The probable meaning is *On the whites of the eyes* or, more generally, *On the eyes*. It seems an improbable subject for the poet-cataloguer, but not an impossible one, and perhaps contact with the considerable body of medical science in Alexandria aroused his interest enough to make a small corner of the field his own.

IV *Conclusion*

We have no means of evaluating Callimachus as a stylist in prose. Some scholars attributed his remark that "a big book is equivalent to a big evil" to the volume *Against Praxiphanes*. If so it might indicate a concision and epigrammatic quality about his prose, which we would expect from his theories of literature generally. But it could equally well have been a thought tossed off in conversation, and it is better to admit our ignorance.

CHAPTER 10

Callimachus: Qualities and Influence

I *Callimachus and Alexandrianism*

CALLIMACHUS was a professional. He was a poet and scholar; more, he was scholar-poet. He was poet because he was scholar, and scholar because he was poet. He commended Aratus as "a poet of outstanding learning and quality" (460). He stood within a literary tradition and was conscious of doing so. In the original introduction to *Aitia* (2) he recalled Hesiod's encounter with the Muses on the mountain of inspiration. Callimachus continually invoked the Muses: it was a part of the tradition. But we should not take it as a mere part of the tradition, as mere poetic coloring; there is no reason to doubt that the Muses were real to the poet.

In the new introduction which he prefaced to his collected works he made the most important statement of his poetic creed, putting it as a revelation from Apollo.

> "My poetic friend, feed up your sacrifices to fatness,
>   keep your Muse slim.
> One further instruction: travel away from the main roads,
>   don't drive your car along routes
> used by others, avoid broad highways, take unfrequented
>   tracks,
>   even if you find them narrow.
> My audience is those who love the cicadas' shrill chirping
>   and loathe the din of donkeys." (1, 23–30)

There are two reasons, then, why Callimachus did not write epic. One is related to his concept of poetry. It is that poetry involves a sustained perfection of craftsmanship which is not possible when

159

the work is on too large a scale. It is not quite the philosophy that
"Small is Beautiful" but it is certainly the philosophy that "Large
is Intractable." Essentially, Callimachus operates on the medium
scale. What is more, he had come up with an answer which our
modern planners, with their cluster colleges (for huge univer-
sities) and satellite towns (for conurbations) are rediscovering in
different contexts; namely, that a large entity is manageable if
and only if you break it into smaller units, each of which has its
own valid unity. It is ironical that *Aitia* is a longer poem than
Apollonius's *Argonautica*.

The other reason has less to do with Callimachus's concept of
poetry than with his sense of his own vocation. This is simply that
everyone was writing epic. There was Apollonius, of course. But,
Apollonius apart, we have literally scores of titles of epics or
quotations from epics written now or later, on mythological
themes, or historical themes, or to glorify the powerful, or to
honor or explore different regions or different peoples.[1] Others
may tread that path, but he will not be with them. If everyone
were writing epyllia or epigrams, Callimachus would not be
doing so. But he was equally not called to take up his machete
and cut a virgin path through the jungle. Apollo summoned him
to existing but unfrequented paths. One fragment runs "I do
nothing without authority" (442). So his independence is a
different dependence from that of others; his originality consists
in new revivals. He expresses this most clearly in his identification of himself with Hipponax at the beginning of *Iambi*. But we
should remember that the *Hymns* too were revivals of the
Homeric hymns. Even if we take a form as obvious as the
epigram, it is easy to forget that Callimachus was a prime shaper
of the Hellenistic epigram. The art never died out: it was anyway
used for sepulchral inscriptions. But no contemporary of
Callimachus, except Leonidas of Tarentum, produced a corpus of
epigrams to compare with his, though his rivals Posidippus and
Aslepiades used the medium. He was building on Simonides and
Plato: he was pointing forward to Meleager and, more distantly,
to Palladas. One aspect of Callimachus's sense of tradition should
be specially mentioned since it is impossible to convey in
translation. This is his use of rare words or phrases to create a
link between his writing and some previous poet. Such allusiveness is a commonplace of ancient poetry. Modern too. Eliot is a
master of it. In Robert Flanagan's "Rerun" a poem about a

western movie ends with the two-word line "Praise him," creating an immediate and unexpected link with Gerard Manley Hopkins's "Pied Beauty." It is an effect that Callimachus frequently controls.

Alexandria has given its name to a style, and Callimachus stands as the supreme exponent of Alexandrianism. Modern critics are suspicious of this term. Still, there was a remarkable literary culture centering on Alexandria between about 280 and 240, and, though Callimachus might not have liked the thought, the things which united the poets of the period were stronger than the things which divided them. We can isolate some of the common features. First, the writers were traditionalists. They might be positively or negatively disposed towards Homer, but if they did not appeal to Homer they appealed to Hesiod or some other. Secondly, they were interested in learning: they were breathing the atmosphere of the Museum and the Library: this is patently true of Aratus, but one can see the same in Theocritus or Apollonius. Thirdly, they were concerned about poetic technique. Callimachus may reasonably have held that a long poem makes sustained technical perfection not merely impossible but in a curious way inappropriate; all the same, Apollonius would have stoutly resisted any impugning of his craftsmanship. Fourthly, they were interested in developing neglected artforms. They were not formally innovatory, except in the minor matter of shaped poems: Callimachus has an epigram, (37) perhaps designed to be inscribed on a quiver: others were to produce similar poems in the shape of an axe, pipe, or egg; they point forward to George Herbert's conceits, or in modern times to some of the verses of Guillaume Apollinaire or Dylan Thomas. But these are trivialities. The revival of neglected forms, dialectic poetry by Aratus, Hymns and Iambi and even lyric poetry by Callimachus, was more in accord with their traditionalism. The forms were sometimes adapted: the epyllion is a good example. Fifthly, although this is not usually cited as a mark of Alexandrianism, they were interested in pouring new wine into the old bottles. This was one of the reasons for taking up forms which were not current at the time; the current forms were not fitted to express the concerns of a new age. There was, for example, an interest in ordinary life, in genre; there was an interest in psychology; there was an interest in the grotesque, the unusual, the unexpected. For it was an imperial, cos-

mopolitan, urban world at Alexandria: even pastoral is to be seen
as an escape from urbanism into an idealized countryside. The
individual, whose identity had been locked up in the community
of the city-state, was now restlessly seeking his new identity. Of
that situation the poets were the interpreters.

II   *Callimachus and the Greeks*

The colossal authority later attaching to the name of
Callimachus makes it easy to see him as a kind of literary
dictator. This he clearly was not. He was a figure of some
importance in the Library, but it is significant that he never
became its Director. He was known at court, and could
contribute state poems on appropriate occasions for Arsinoe's
wedding, and for Ptolemy's death and deification in the 270s, for
Berenice's act of dedication and Sosibius's victories in the games
in the 240s. But there are touches of flattery which suggest that
he was less than assured.

Among his literary contemporaries he was in a state of
alienation. We do not see him as the center of a literary clique.
He gives the impression of walking by himself. He was subject to
attack from Posidippus, Asclepiades, Praxiphanes, and their
followers; they are the Telchines. We do not know what the
quarrel was about, but we do know that they admired
Antimachus and he did not. His reply is so violent that we can
sense a feeling of vulnerability; he is on the defensive. His
relationship with Apollonius is unclear. There is some ancient
authority for saying that they were in opposition to one another.
Some modern scholars think that this arose from a false
deduction that Callimachus's opposition to epic must have been
directed against the leading contemporary epic poet. Still, we
should be cautious about such scepticism: after all, Callimachus
did criticize epic and Apollonius did write epic: and the ancient
authorities did have access to sources which we have lost. To
Apollonius is attributed a hostile epigram:

> Callimachus: muck, trifle, blockhead.
> Original: Callimachus for writing *Origins*. (*AP* 11, 275)

There is an ingenious suggestion that the first line is based on an
alphabetical dictionary which would run

KALLIMACHOS:
[KALLUSMA]: muck
[KALLOPISMA]: trifle
[KALOPOUS]: wooden leg

("Blockhead" by substituting *NOUS* for *POUS*). In the second line the work is' of course *Aitia*, and *aitios* (here rendered "original" i.e., "odd" to keep the pun) is the ordinary Greek for "guilty." Further, the Telchines were associated with Rhodes, which would fit Apollonius. Apollonius, however, was not above learning from Callimachus; nor was Theocritus, an altogether greater poet.

One close follower of Callimachus, and pupil of his, was his fellow-townsman Philostephanus of Cyrene, who wrote a highly Callimachean poem on *The Rivers of the World*. Callimachus's chief disciple, however, was Euphorion. Euphorion was not a negligible figure, and Cicero can call the Latin modernists of his own day "Euphorion's singers." Elsewhere he calls Euphorion an excessively obscure writer.[2] Euphorion, like Callimachus, was fascinated by mythology, by legends attaching to places, by tracing the mythological explanation *(aition)* of cult-practice. He was also an exponent of the epyllion, as a medium for the portrayal of violent love. But he was not primarily interested in the story; he was interested, like Apollonius, in feminine psychology, and, like Callimachus, in learned allusion. When Apriate escapes the attentions of Trambelus by suicide her farewell speech is long and learned, her death mercifully short.[3]

Two poets of the Hellenistic Age owed a particular debt to Callimachus. One is Moschus. We see him in the traditions of pastoral poetry to which Callimachus made no special contribution. But *Europa* is a typical epyllion, telling the story briefly, but dwelling on aspects which are inventive and intrinsically interesting—a dream which gives Europa a premonition of what is to come, the flower-basket and on it the story of Io (a relevant parallel), the ironical tenderness of the girl for the bull, the brilliantly baroque account of their journey through the waves.

The other is Parthenius, a neglected poet of the first century B.C.[4] Little enough survives, but we know him as a collector of curious lore: he called the river Satrachus by the name Aoos, which itself is a somewhat out-of-the-way name for Adonis. We know that he was interested in mythology, wrote about Adonis,

and indeed compiled a *Metamorphoses*. We know that, like
Euphorion, he was interested in unhappy and abnormal love. He
put together a series of such stories for Cornelius Gallus, and
quoted some verses he had himself written on the incestuous
love of Byblis for her brother Caunus. They are described as
Callimachean, and indeed they have all his mentor's burnished
care, carefully structured, un-Homeric:

> When she recognized her fatal brother's intention
> she cried more unceasingly than nightingales within a thicket
> mourning over and again for the boy from Sithon.
> Quickly she fastened her girdle to a gnarled oak
> and fashioned a noose. For her
> girls of Miletus tore their clothes.

Plainly he espoused the short story in verse, the epyllion, and in
fact he spoke in criticism of Homer, as Callimachus never did,
calling *The Iliad* "muck" and *The Odyssey* "mud."

Meleager was another who appreciated Callimachus, and
owed him some debt, incorporating some of his epigrams into
The Garland. He wrote, in his brief characterizations, of
Callimachus's "astringent honey." Meleager himself was a minor
poet, derivative but not without charm; he included some 130 of
his own verses in *The Garland*.

Meleager ensured that as long as there was an interest in
Greek verse something of Callimachus would survive as poetry,
and Callimachus is well represented in the Palatine Anthology
by over sixty pieces. But the extraordinary range of those who
refer to him or quote him shows his continuing influence: they
include Athenaeus, Stobaeus, and *The Suda* of course; Strabo and
Plutarch and Galen and Lucian and Diogenes Laertius and
Artemidorus and Aelian; Clement of Alexandria (several times);
commentators, both Greek and Latin, Eustratius and Servius and
Probus, and innumerable scholiasts; lexicons such as the
Etymologicum Magnum and Stephanus of Byzantium. And the
considerable fragments of papyrus showed that he continued to
be read in his own Egypt.

III   *Callimachus and Roman Poetry*

At the beginning of Latin poetry stands the towering figure of
Ennius. It is quite certain that Ennius, a man of learning who

grew up in an area of Greek culture and was intimate with Greek poetry, knew Callimachus's work. He opened his epic *Annals* not with an invocation to the Muses, but with a dream of Homer appearing to him and explaining that, in accordance with Pythagoras's views on metempsychosis, his soul had inherited the body, not of a wildfowl, but of a peacock, and had now passed into Ennius's body. Nothing in Callimachus's work was more familiar than the Hesiodic dream with which he began the original version of *Aitia;* nothing is more certain than that Ennius is deliberately alluding to this. But Ennius was writing a very un-Callimachean poem, and his inspiration was the Homer whom Callimachus had deliberately disowned. Wendell Clausen must be right in saying that Ennius is alluding to the passage in Callimachus precisely in order to repudiate the latter's view of poetry.[5] But Clausen underestimates the extent to which one may repudiate a poet and still be influenced by him. Ennius was interested in what contemporary Greek poets were doing, and what they were doing was broadly Callimachean. Indeed, it is, ironically, Callimachean to introduce literary polemic without naming one's opponent, as Ennius does here and at the beginning of Book 7. In the very diversity of his poetic interests Ennius resembles Callimachus and no other poet. A good case has been made out that Callimachus's *Iambi* influenced the beginning of Roman satire in Ennius, and especially Lucilius;[6] to rebut this, as Clausen does, by saying that "the *Iambi* was, in Latin poetry, one of Callimachus' least consequential works" is to beg the question.

The Latin elegiac writers of the second and start of the first century B.C. were aware of Callimachus, without being closely indebted to him: Lutatius Catulus translated one of his epigrams into Latin. Callimachus came into his own with the circle around Valerius Cato, "the Latin Siren," which included Catullus, Calvus, Helvius Cinna, Furius Bibaculus, and others. Clausen has persuasively suggested that the source of the new enthusiasm for Callimachus lay in no one other than Parthenius, who, according to *The Suda,* came to Rome as prisoner-of-war somewhere about 73 B.C., was given over to one Cinna, presumably a relation of Helvius Cinna, and subsequently freed on account of his learning. Helvius Cinna wrote a poem called *Zmyrna,* on a theme of incestuous passion which may well have been derived from Parthenius. Catullus in a polished and polemical epigram (95), very Callimachean, celebrated it for its polish over nine years,

and its brevity, and contrasted the long wordy works of
Hortensius and Volusius. Cinna's poem will travel to the river
Satrachus it celebrates: we have already seen that Parthenius
celebrated the same river, which is seldom mentioned elsewhere: Volusius's will perish by his own Po. Clausen points out
that the comparison between a large sluggish river with its
flotsam and jetsam and a pure swift-flowing stream is derived
from Callimachus (*Hymn* 2, 108-12). Cinna's poem was an
epyllion, so was Calvus's *Io*. So was Catullus's *Peleus and Thetis*.
Catullus had other affinities with Callimachus: his learning,
which was not inconsiderable; his polish, which controlled
seemingly ingenuous passages; his experiments with meter; his
use of meters for types of poetry for which they were not
traditionally employed; his use of conversational language; his
polemics. And Catullus translated *The Lock of Berenice* in a
period of depression when his mind would not cope with creative
writing; it is significant of much that this was his choice.

Parthenius's influence extended beyond Valerius Cato's circle
to the poets of the next generation, in particular Cornelius Gallus
and young Vergil. For Gallus, as we noted, he suggested
mythological themes for erotic elegy. More, we know from
Servius[7] that Gallus adapted into Latin a poem by Euphorion,
presumably aetiological, on the Grynean grove, perhaps bor-
rowing from Parthenius himself as well. As for Vergil, Macrobius
tells us that Parthenius tutored him in Greek. Clausen has shown
that the sixth eclogue is a declaration of poetic intent. Vergil
refuses to write about war. Part of his motive is Epicurean
pacifism, but the other part is Callimachus's rejection of epic.
Vergil will use a slender pipe to cultivate his muse. He is writing
Theocritean pastoral according to Callimachean poetical theory.
By the time he wrote *The Georgics* (and a didactic poem was a
natural outcome of Callimachean principles) he was beginning to
change, but in the second book he makes a Callimachean claim to
be opening unsullied springs, and to be singing Hesiodic (that is,
Callimachean) strains, and the Aristaeus episode at the end
incorporates the epyllion of Orpheus and Eurydice. Only with
The Aeneid has Vergil moved right away from Callimachus; he
was not satisfied with it and wanted to burn it, and Clausen
ventures the thought that, just possibly, some Callimachean
scruples haunted him to the end.

Of the other Augustan poets, Propertius and Ovid were the most Callimachean. Propertius actually invoked Callimachus:

> Shades of Callimachus and Rites of Philitas of Cos,
> please admit me to your grove.
> I am the first to process, a priest from a pure spring,
> celebrating Italian festivals in Greek song.
> (3, 1, 1-4 cf 3, 9, 43-4; 4, 1, 64; 4, 6, 4)

The purity of his sources was something on which Callimachus insisted. In this connection the opening of Propertius's first poem is of interest:

> Cynthia was the first to capture my heart with her eyes:
> desire had never touched me before. (1, 1-2)

It is wholly Callimachean in its directness. Within a very few lines we are reading

> Tullus, Milanion, by accepting every trial, broke through
> the cruelty of Iasus's hard-hearted daughter. (1, 9-10)

which is equally Callimachean in its allusiveness. There are many echoes of Callimachus in Propertius, including "The Dream"; the fourth book particularly is a conscious application of Callimachean aetiology to Roman institutions; not for nothing was he called "the Roman Callimachus".

Ovid, too, is highly Callimachean. Patrick Wilkinson wrote of him: "More important, however, is the influence of the Kallimachean spirit. Many readers of the *Metamorphoses* have been baffled by the shifts of mood and subject, between romance, rhetoric, burlesque, pathos, macabre, grotesque, patriotism, landscape, genre, antiquarianism . . . Now this *poikilia,* this variety of mood, is thoroughly Alexandrian, and particularly characteristic of the versatile and mischievous genius of Kallimachos."[8] *Metamorphoses* is in fact a collection of epyllia. *Ibis* was derived directly from Callimachus in title and conception, though not in detail. *Fasti,* though it takes its structure from the logic of the calendar, is in other ways close to *Aitia.* Mario de Cola has shown that Ovid draws on Callimachus, sometimes for broad ideas, sometimes for detailed phrases, even in the poems of his youth. Ovid said of Callimachus that he made up in professional skill what he lacked in natural ability;[9] he was certainly willing to take lessons from that skill; Sullivan calls him the last of the neo-Callimacheans.[10]

Later in the first century A.D. there are signs of Callimachus's continued favor with Roman readers. The encyclopaedic Pliny was familiar with *Hecale,* and if he shows no appreciation of it as poetry he gleans from it references to vegetables, sow-thistles, both white and black, and sea-fennel.[11] More telling is a passage in Martial:

> You won't find Centaurs, Gorgons, Harpies here:
>   my page smacks of man.
> But, Mamurra, you've no wish to know your own character,
>   your self: read Callimachus's *Aitia.* (10, 4, 9–12)

The point is not the reference itself, which is part of Martial's satire: it is that Martial expected the reference to be appreciated and enjoyed. And we have seen Martial's appreciation of Callimachus's qualities as an epigrammatist.

IV   *Callimachus and Later Poetry*

Except for the *Hymns,* which were first printed in Florence in 1494, and the anthologized epigrams (printed with the *Hymns* in 1566), Callimachus's poetry did not survive the Middle Ages, and he had little impact on the Renaissance: indeed he has had little direct influence upon subsequent European and American literature. The one major poet on whom there is a direct discernible influence is Pierre de Ronsard. He was one of the group of seven poets who called themselves the Pléiade, using the vernacular to blend French and Graeco-Roman traditions. The same name had been used by a group of poets in third-century Alexandria, though Callimachus was not one of their number. Ronsard had been instructed by a teacher of genius, Jean Dorat or D'Aurat, and put in touch with poets who were outside the general curriculum: this was how he came to know Callimachus's *Hymns.* The great influences on his poetry were Pindar and Horace. It was his boast to rival Pindar and surpass Horace; this was not justified, and he was on surer ground when he claimed to be both the French Horace and the French Pindar.

But his *Hymns* are much indebted to Callimachus, and by the
1550s he had turned away from Pindar, and was looking to the
Greek Anthology, which influenced his sonnets. Ronsard further
paraphrased in verse a passage from *Aitia* quoted by Stobaeus:

> Toute la viande qui entre
> Dans la gouffre ingrat de ce ventre
> Incontinent sans fruit resort.
> Mais la belle science exquise
> Que par l'ouye j'ay apprise
> M'accompagne jusq'à la mort.

This is a version of a passage near the start of the second book:

> Assuredly all that I then gave to my head—
>   smooth golden ointments with scented flowers—
> all speedily lost their scent; of all that passed my teeth,
>   sunk in my ungracious belly,
> nothing remained till next day; the only things I kept
>   are what entered my ears. (43, 12-7)

Even translation has not produced much. There is no adequate
translation of the *Hymns,* and the *Epigrams* have produced only
one memorable version. This is in William Johnson Cory's *Ionica*
(1858) and is rightly famous: it has been well set musically by C.
V. Stanford.

> They told me, Heraclitus, they told me you were dead;
> They brought me bitter news to hear and bitter tears to shed.
> I wept, as I remember'd how often you and I
> Had tired the sun with talking and sent him down the sky.
> And now that thou art lying, my dear old Carian guest,
> A handful of grey ashes, long, long ago at rest,
> Still are thy pleasant voices, thy nightingales, awake,
> For Death, he taketh all away, but them he cannot take.

It has been well said that the translation possesses almost every
grace except that of the original. For Cory takes 44 words where
Callimachus takes 17 or 18; he says everything twice; he is
extravagant where Callimachus is economical, and effusive
where Callimachus is restrained.

But if the direct influence of Callimachus has been minimal

there has been from time to time across the history of poetry an assertion of Callimachean values. One example will suffice. T. S. Eliot is the most Callimachean of poets. Like Callimachus, he is a learned poet, and his poetry is in his learning, and his learning in his poetry. *The Waste Land* to all intents and purposes needed his notes before it could be read at all. Like Callimachus, he is fascinated by mythology (it permeates *The Waste Land* and *The Four Quartets;* it is most obvious in his plays, not merely in *Murder in the Cathedral* which is an exploration of the Becket myth, but in his secular dramas with their analogues in Greek myth). Like Callimachus, he believes in the short poem, or rather disbelieves in the long poem, though *The Four Quartets* shows him, like Callimachus in *Aitia,* organizing subsections into a larger whole. Like Callimachus, he is interested in aetiology. Like Callimachus, he espoused a variety of metrical patterns and forms of poetry. Like Callimachus, he is both an innovator and a traditionalist. Like Callimachus, he has a peculiar genius for linking together the homely and the timeless: witness Prufrock or Sweeney. Like Callimachus, he knows how to mingle conversational language with learned artifice. Like Callimachus, he can strike out the memorable phrase. Like Callimachus, he is a keen and exact observer, often of seemingly insignificant detail which becomes, as he presents it, important and revealing. Like Callimachus, he is a supreme craftsman, who goes to immense pains over his work, who believes in the labor of the file, the patient whittling and polishing. Like Callimachus, although he works on a relatively small scale, he is not just a miniaturist (like Landor or Housman), but a "high poet."

So Callimachus lives on. He is not everyone's poet. His learning becomes tedious: this is not just because it has lost its immediacy, for it would have been obscure to his own generation. But it is a part of him; we cannot discard it and must not dismiss it. He lives on because the values by which he wrote are genuine poetic values. They are not the only poetic values. They may not be the most important; that is a matter for debate. But they are real. And the values once admitted, he remains one of their supreme exponents.

Notes and References

Chapter One

1. M. Cary, *A History of the Greek World 323-146 B.C.* (London, ²1951), p. 291.
2. *Berliner Klassikertexte* Fasc. 7, pp. 17, 28.
3. G. Sarton, *A History of Science* (New York, 1959), p. 155.
4. A convenient account will be found in R. Goodchild, *Cyrene and Apollonia* (United Kingdom of Libya Antiquities Department of Cyrenaica 1959).
5. Jos. *Ant.* 14,115 ff.

Chapter Two

1. Catullus 95,10; Propertius 3,1,1. Rudolf Pfeiffer took a different view of the contrasts and held that Callimachus was comparing the shorter poems of Mimnermus and Philitas favorably with their own longer poems. The word *nightingales* was suggested for the mutilated part of the text by A.E. Housman: compare *Epig.* 2,5.
2. Plato, *Phaedr.* 259; Theocr. 1,148; *Anth. Pal* 12,98; Ps-Anac. 34 Bergk.
3. Fragment 2,5; Hes. *WD* 265.
4. F. Jacoby, *Fragmenta Graecorum Historicorum* iii B, pp. 7-10.
5. Ap. Rhod. 4,1694 ff.; Apollod. *Lib.* 1,9,26,2.
6. *P. Oxy.* 2263.
7. The Busiris Vase in Vienna, from Caere, though not made there.
8. Thue. 5,84-6,1 tells the story with power; it was for him the turning-point of the war, the tragic wrong which led to the fall of Athens. Euripides wrote *The Women of Troy* to expose this military ruthlessness.
9. Published by C. Meillier *Cahiers de Recherches de l'Institut de Papyrologie et d'Egyptologie de Lille* 4(1976) and discussed by P.J. Parsons *Zeitschrift für Papyrologie und Epigraphik* 25(1977) 1-50.
10. Cf. Simon. fragment 78D.
11. F. Jacoby, *FGH* iii B, pp. 7-10 add. p. 757.
12. See also Ovid, *Her.* 20; 21; Aristaenetus, *Ep.* 1,10.
13. Compare Augustine's amazement at finding Ambrose reading soundlessly *Conf.* 6,3.

14. Hippocr. *Sacred Disease* 1.
15. See R. Pfeiffer, "The Image of the Delian Apollo and Apolline Ethics," *J. Warburg and Courtauld Inst.* 15 (1952), 21 ff.
16. Paus. 6,6,11.
17. In his supplementary chapter to Couat.
18. H.J. Rose, *A History of Greek Literature* (London, 1934), p. 319.
19. T.B.L. Webster, *Hellenistic Poetry and Art* (London, 1964), pp. 119-20.

Chapter Three

1. For these see G.A. Gerhard, *Phoinix von Kolophon* (Leipzig, 1909).
2. Diog, Laert. 1,28.
3. B.R. Rees in *Class. Rev.* 75 (1961), 1.
4. *Fab.* 383 H. Philo *Confus. Ling.*, 6 ff. has a version derived from Callimachus.
5. See Ap. Rhod. 4,1756 ff.
6. Hdt. 2,51.
7. F. Jacoby, *FGH* iii B, p. 642.
8. A von Blumenthal, *Ion von Chios*, Stuttgart 1939; F. Jacoby in *Class. Quart.* 41 (1947), 1 ff.

Chapter Four

1. Ath. 15,667D,668D.

Chapter Five

1. *Epig.* 6.
2. Schol. ad Callim. *Hymn* 2,106.
3. E.g. Ov.*Met.* 8,620 ff.; [Verg.] *Moretum.*
4. Plut. *Thes.* 14: from Philochorus.
5. Ov. *Met.* 8, 1 ff.
6. J.U. Powell, *Collectanea Alexandrina*, (Oxford 1925) pp. 72 ff.
7. *Berliner Klassische Texte* 1,57.

Chapter Six

1. Ath. 7,284 C.
2. Theocr. 11; Callim. *Epig.* 46,1.
3. Hdt. 1,165.
4. Epig. 28; *Hymn* 2,111 cf. Prop. 3,1,3 *puro de fonte.*

Chapter Seven

1. 3,237 is an exception.
2. See M.T. Smiley in *Hermathena* 18 (1919), 46–69.
3. For the negative analysis see E. Cahen, *Callimaque*, pp. 247 ff., though his own conclusion is equally unacceptable.
4. Justin 16,2, 7.
5. Hes. *Theog.* 96.
6. See also Paus. 1, 7, 2.
7. Gal. 3,1.
8. It is possible that the Palladium was in the temple of Athene Akria.
9. T.S. Eliot, "The Waste Land" in *Complete Poems and Plays* (London 1969).

Chapter Eight

1. G. Kaibel, *Epigrammata Graeca ex lapidibus collecta* (Berlin, 1878); W. Peek, *Griechische Vers-Inschriften*, 2 vols. (Berlin, 1955–60).
2. See G. Giangrande, "Callimachus, Poetry and Love," *Eranos* 67 (1969), 33–42.
3. Hor. *AP* 242.
4. Hor. *Sat.* 1,2,105.
5. Mart. 4,23.

Chapter Nine

1. *P. Oxy.* 23,2368.
2. C.O. Brink in *CQ* 40 (1946), 16 ff.

Chapter Ten

1. K. Ziegler, *Das hellenistische Epos* (Leipzig, 1934).
2. Cic. *Div.* 2,64.
3. D.L. Page, *Select Papyri* (Loeb), III, 494–97.
4. The fragments were collected by Martini.
5. W. Clausen, "Callimachus and Roman Poetry," *GRBS* 5 (1964), 181–96.
6. M. Puelma Piwonka, *Lucilius und Kallimachos* (Frankfurt, 1949).
7. Ad Verg. *Ecl.* 6,72.
8. In *Fondation Hardt: Entretiens* II, p. 237.

9. Ov. *Am.* 1, 15,14.
10. J.P. Sullivan, *Propertius* (Cambridge, 1976), p. 114.
11. Plin. *NH* 22,88; 26,82.

Selected Bibliography

PRIMARY SOURCES

Cahen, E. *Callimaque.* Paris: Les Belles Lettres,³ 1948. Good edition with French translation and some notes, but pre-Pfeiffer.

Gow, A.S.F. and Page, D.L. The Greek Anthology: *Hellenistic Epigrams.* 2 vols. Cambridge, England: University Press, 1965. Useful for text of epigrams.

Howald, E. and Staiger, E. *Die Dichtungen des Kallimachos.* Zürich: Artemis-Verlag, 1955.

Mair, A.W. *Callimachus and Lycophron* and Mair, G. W. *Aratus.* London: Heinemann; New York: Putnam, 1921. A joint volume in the Loeb series: the Callimachus section contains Hymns, Epigrams, and some fragments with an English translation.

Pfeiffer, R. *Callimachus.* 2 vols. Oxford: Clarendon Press, Vol I,² 1949; Vol II, 1953. This great edition makes all previous work outmoded.

Trypanis, C.A. *Callimachus: Fragments.* London: Heinemann; Cambridge (Mass.): Harvard University Press, 1958. In the Loeb series, omitting Hymns and Epigrams. An excellent text and translation with useful notes.

SECONDARY SOURCES

1. General Background

On history:

COOK, S.A., ADCOCK, F.E. and CHARLESWORTH, M.P. (eds.) *The Hellenistic Monarchies and the Rise of Rome.* Vol. 7 in *Cambridge Ancient History.* Cambridge, England: University Press, 1928.

FERGUSON, J. *The Heritage of Hellenism.* London: Thames and Hudson, 1973.

ROSTOVTZEFF, M. I. *A Social and Economic History of the Hellenistic World.* 3 vols. Oxford: Clarendon Press, 1941. Monumental and standard.

TARN, W. W. *Hellenistic Civilization.* Cleveland and New York: Meridian Books,³ 1961.

175

On Alexandria:
FRASER, P. M. *Ptolemaic Alexandria*. 2 vols. Oxford: Clarendon Press, 1972. This includes a useful chapter on Callimachus, and is generally essential.
PARSONS, E. A. *The Alexandrian Library*. London: Cleaver-Hume Press, 1952. This is not wholly satisfactory, but remains useful.

On the scholarly activity of the period:
PFEIFFER, R. *History of Classical Scholarship*. Oxford: Clarendon Press, 1968. Essential.
SARTON, G. *A History of Science*. London: Oxford University Press, 1959.

2. Hellenistic Poetry

COUAT, A. *Alexandrian Poetry Under the First Three Ptolemies* E.T. London: Heinemann, 1931. Mellifluous and still useful.
KÖRTE, A. *Hellenistic Poetry* E.T. New York: Columbia University Press, 1929.
LEGRAND, Ph.-E. *La Poèsie Alexandrine*. Paris: Ccllection Payot, 1928.
LESKY, A. *A History of Greek Literature*. E.T. London: Methuen, 1966. The standard general history. The relevant sections are excellent.
ROSTAGNI, A. *Poeti Alessandrini*. Turin: Bocca, 1916.
SUSEMIHL, F. *Geschichte der griechischen Literatur in der Alexandrinerzeit*. 2 vols. Leipzig: Rubner, 1891-2. Less discerning and original than Wilamowitz, but scholarly and thorough.
WEBSTER, T. B. L. *Hellenistic Poetry and Art*. London: Methuen, 1964. An original and suggestive book, taking account of recent scholarly work, bringing together society, art, and literature, and containing an admirable chapter on Callimachus.
WILAMOWITZ-MOELLENDORFF, U. VON *Hellenistische Dichtung in der Zeit des Kallimachos*. 2 vols. Berlin: Weidmannsche Buchhandlung, 1927. Though pre-Pfeiffer this remains one of the great works of scholarship and insight.

3. Callimachus: General

CAHEN, E. *Callimaque et son oeuvre poetique*. Paris: de Boccard, 1929. A 650-page monograph, learned and useful in its day, but outmoded by Pfeiffer's edition.
CAPOVILLA, G. *Callimaco*. 2 vols. Rome: L'Erma, 1967. This enormous work, running to over 1100 pages, is the most recent full treatment, but alas! is cited here as a warning, as it is thoroughly unsatisfactory.

HERTER, H. *"Kallimachos."* in Pauly, M. and Wissowa, G, (eds) *Real-Encyclopädie der klassischen Alterthumswissenschaft* (Stuttgart and Munich 1894-) suppl., vol. xiii. (1973) An indispensable up-to-date survey.

HOWALD, E. *Der Dichter Kallimachos von Kyrene.* Zürich: Rentsch, 1943. Pre-Pfeiffer, but a quite charming brief appreciation.

SKIADAS, A. D., ed. *Kallimachos.* Darmstadt: Wissenschaftliche Buchgesellschaft, 1975. A valuable collection of papers. This contains an up-to-date bibliography.

4. Callimachus: Studies of individual works

CLAYMAN, D. L. *"Callimachus' Iambi (Mnemosyne* Supplement 59) Leiden: E.J. Brill 1980.

On Iambi:

DAWSON, C. M. "The Iambi of Callimachus." *Yale Classical Studies* 11(1950), 1-68.

On Hymns:

CAHEN, C. *Les Hymnes de Callimaque: Commentaire explicatif et critique.* Paris: de Boccard, 1930. The most useful single general critical appreciation, though not wholly satisfactory.

HUSSEY, W. D. "Politics and Poetry in the First Two Hymns of Callimachus". Diss. Ohio, 1973. A useful examination of the political element in the first two hymns.

On Hymn 1:

MCLENNAN, G. *Callimachus: Hymn to Zeus: Introduction and Commentary.* Rome: Edizioni dell' Ateneo e Bizarri, 1977. A valuable edition and commentary, which reached me too late to use.

On Hymn 2:

ERBSE, H. "Zum Apollonhymnos des Kallimachos." *Hermes* 83 (1955), 411-28.

WILLIAMS, F. *Callimachus: Hymn to Apollo: A Commentary.* Oxford: Clarendon Press, 1978. A valuable edition and commentary, which reached me too late to use.

On Hymn 3:

BORNEMANN, F. *Callimachus: Hymnus in Dianam.* Florence: La Nuova Italia, 1968.

On Hymn 4:
McKAY. K. J. "Crime and Punishment in Kallimachos' *Hymn to Delos*"
Antichthon 3(1969) 127-9.

On Hymn 5:
KLEINKNECHT. H. "Loutra Tes Pallados." *Hermes* 74 (1934), 301-50.
McKAY. K. J. *The Poet at Play: Kallimachos, The Bath of Pallas*
(*Mnemosyne* Supp. 6). Leiden, 1962.

On Hymn 6:
BULLOCH. A. W. "Callimachus *Erysichthon*, Homer and Apollonius
Rhodius." *American Journal of Philology* 98(1977), 97-123.
McKAY. K. J. *Erysichthon: A Callimachean Comedy* (*Mnemosyne* Supp.
7). Leiden, 1962.

On Epigrams:
BUM. F. *Die Epigramme des Kallimachos*. Diss. Wien, 1940.
FERGUSON. J. "The Epigrams of Callimachus". *Greece and Rome* 17
(1970), 64-80.

On *Hecale* and the epyllion generally:
ALLEN. W, JR. "The Epyllion." *Transactions and Proceedings of
American Philological Association.* 71 (1940), 1-26.
CRUMP. M. M. *The Epyllion from Theocritus to Ovid*. Oxford, 1931.
NEWMAN. J. K. "Callimachus and the Epic" in Heller, J. L., ed. *Serta
Turyniana* pp. 342-60. Urbana: University of Illinois Press, 1974.

On *Aitia:*
KLEIN. T. M. "Callimachus and the Counter-Genre." *Latomus* 33 (1974),
217-31.
SWIDEREK. A. "La structure des Aitia de Callimaque à la lumière des
nouvelles découvertes papyrologiques." *Journal of Juristic
Papyrology* 5 (1951), 229-35.

On *Pinax:*
BLUM. R. *Kallimachos und die Literaturverzeichnung bei den Griechen*.
Frankfurt: Buchhandler-Vereinigung, 1977.

5. Callimachus: Particular Aspects

CARRIERE. J. "L'effet de double coupe dans l'hexamètre de Callimaque."
Pallas 5 (1957), 5-15. This is a sensitive study of a particular
metrical effect.

DEL GRANDE, C. "Espressione Callimachea e Tradizione di Forma Lirica" *Filologia Minore.* Milan and Naples: Ricciardi, 1956. chapter 23 This has a useful collection of material on the poet's use of language.

REINSCH-WERNER, H. *Callimachus Hesiodicus.* Berlin: Verlag Nikolaus Mielke, 1976. A study of the influence of Hesiod on the poet.

STAEHELIN, H. "Die Religion des Kallimachos." Diss. Zürich, 1934. On the poet's religion.

ZEIGLER, K. "Kallimachos und die Frauen." *Die Antike* 13 (1937), 20–42. On the poet's handling of the theme of love.

6. Influence

CLAUSEN, W. V. "Callimachus and Roman poetry." *Greek, Roman and Byzantine Studies* 5 (1965), 193 ff. Original and valuable.

COLA, M. DE *Callimaco e Ovidio.* Palermo: Trimarchi, 1937.

GEORGE, E. V. *Aeneid VIII and the Aitia of Callimachus.* Leiden: Brill, 1974.

PILLINGER, H. E. "Some Callimachean influences in Propertius, Book 4". *Harvard Studies in Classical Philology* 73 (1969), 171–99.

PIWONKA PUELMA, M. *Lucilius and Kallimachos.* Frankfurt: Klostermann. 1949. A book that ranges widely and importantly.

SULLIVAN, J. P. *Propertius: A Critical Introduction.* Cambridge: University Press, 1976. Provoking and stimulating.

WIMMEL, W. *Kallimachos in Rom.* (Hermes Einzelschr. 16) Wiesbaden: Franz Steiner Verlag GMBH, 1960. An essential book.

Index

180

DATE DUE			

DEMCO 38-297